Evil Penguins
When Cute Penguins Go Bad

Elia Anie

***What's black-and-white and evil all over? This hilarious
cartoon book reveals the terrifying truth. . . .***

Penguins. They're everywhere—gracing movie screens, Coke ads, and
merchandise. But don't let those happy feet fool you. When they're not
surfing or marching bravely across the Antarctic, penguins have a whole other
agenda. And it isn't pretty. In *Evil Penguins*, Elia Anie captures the antics of cute
little birds who have gone over to the dark side. Here are cartoons of penguins
leading revolts, giving SpongeBob a swirly, causing plagues, clubbing baby seals,
killing Inuits while dressed as ninjas, and wreaking havoc in dozens of other
hysterically appalling ways. If you thought the worst a penguin could do is make
you feel guilty about global warming, think again. Poised to become a dark humor
classic in the deliciously nasty tradition of *The Book of Bunny Suicides* and *101 Uses
for a Dead Cat*, this is a perfect gift book and a must-have for both penguin lovers
and those who know that evil can come in even the cuddliest packages.

ELIA ANIE's love of penguins has led her to Antarctica, the Falkland Islands, the
Galapagos, and Australia. Her photographs of penguins have appeared in *Popular
Photography* and *The Galapagos Conservancy*. This is her first book.

Nonfiction
Trade Paperback Original
September 2008
$10.00U.S./$11.50 Can.
1-4169-6115-1 • 978-1-4169-6115-4
96 pages • 7 x 5

EVIL PENGUINS

WHEN CUTE PENGUINS GO BAD

by elia anie

SSE

SIMON SPOTLIGHT ENTERTAINMENT
New York London Toronto Sydney

To misunderstood penguins everywhere. . . .

Deepest gratitude to my agent, Michelle Bower, my editor;
Emily Westlake, for believing in my misbehaving penguins;
and to my other half, whose trust in my craziness
has made this book possible.

S|S|E

Simon Spotlight Entertainment
A Division of Simon & Schuster, Inc.
1230 Avenue of the Americas
New York, NY 10020

Copyright © 2008 by Elia Anie

First Simon Spotlight Entertainment trade paperback edition September 2008

SIMON SPOTLIGHT ENTERTAINMENT and colophon
are trademarks of Simon & Schuster, Inc.

For information about special discounts for bulk purchases,
please contact Simon & Schuster Special Sales at
1-800-456-6798 or business@simonandschuster.com.

Manufactured in the United States America

10 9 8 7 6 5 4 3 2 1

Library of Congress Cataloging-in-Publication Data tk

ISBN-13:978-1-4169-6115-4
ISBN-10:   1-4169-6115-1

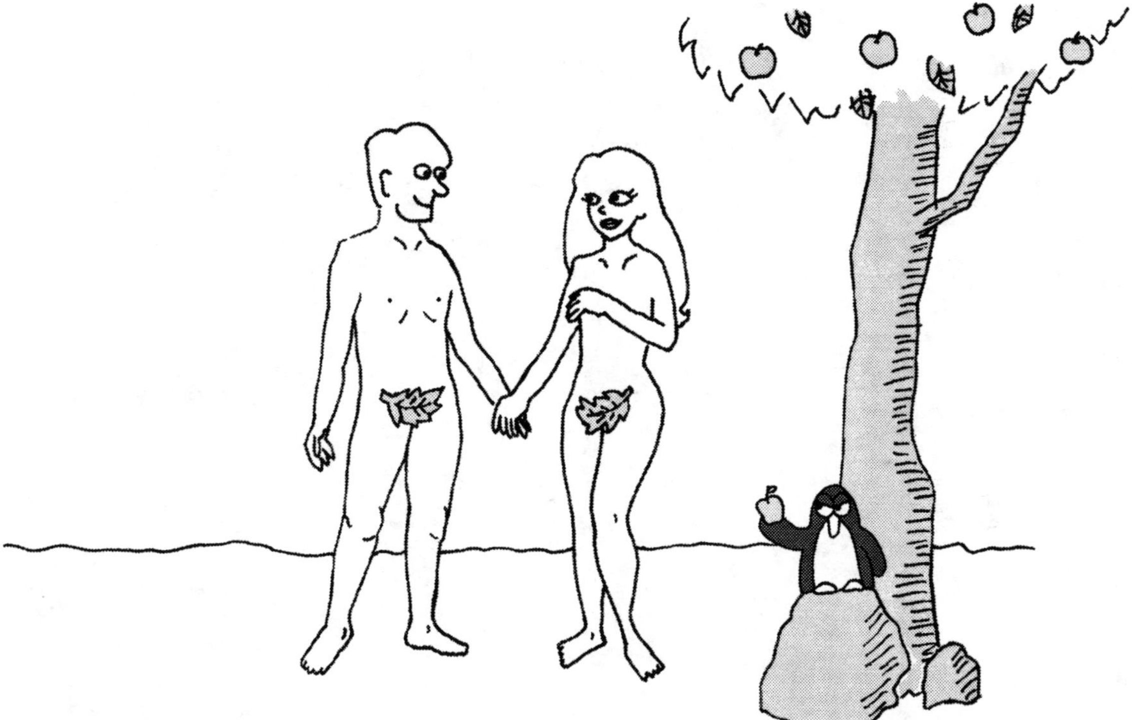

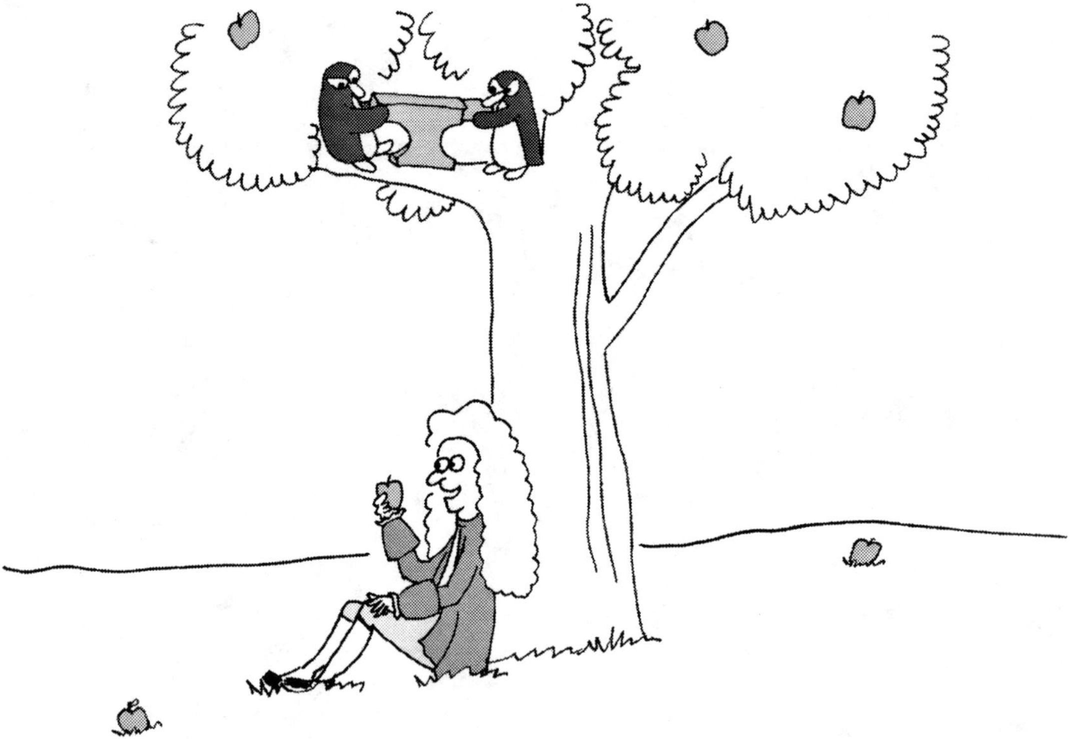

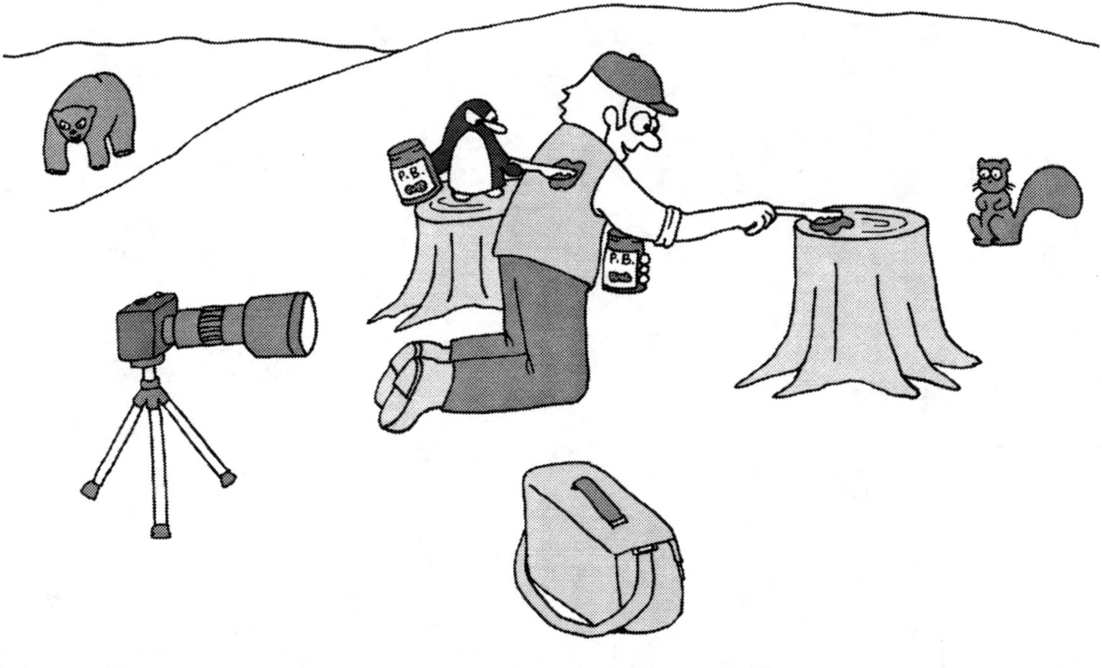
P.B.
P.B.

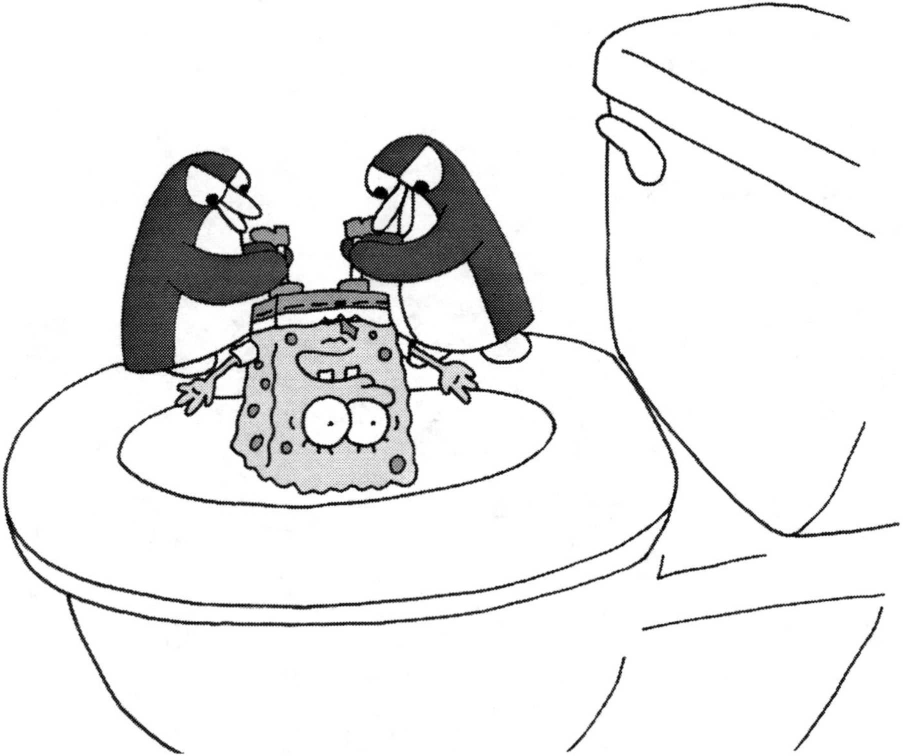

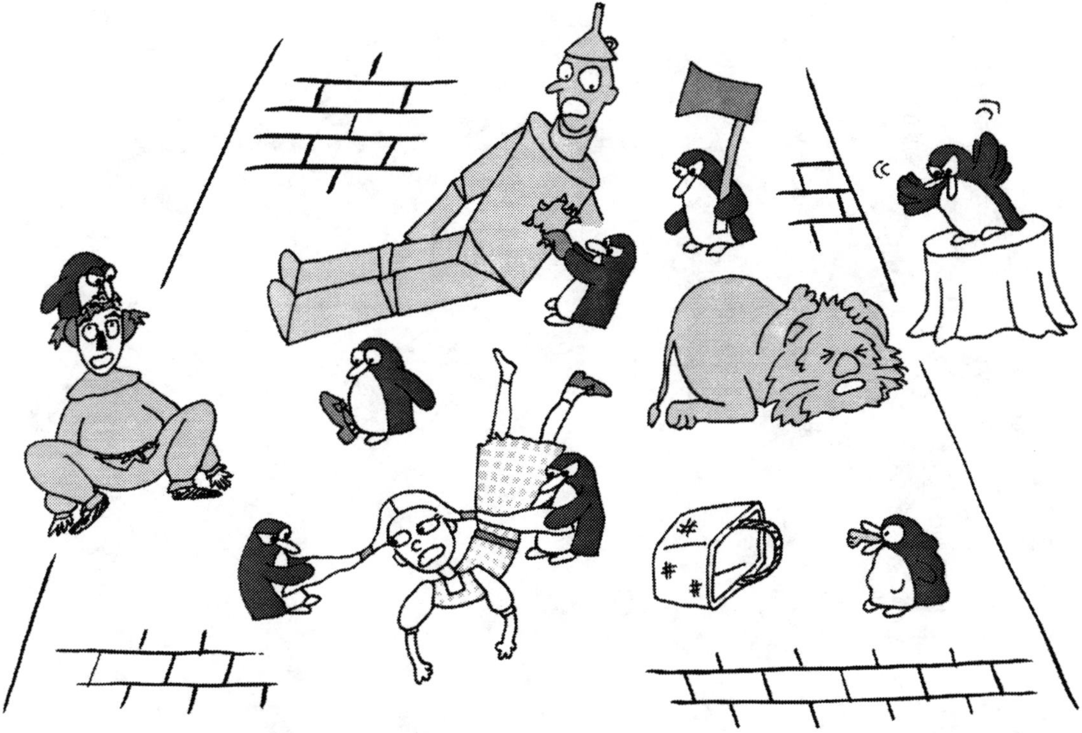

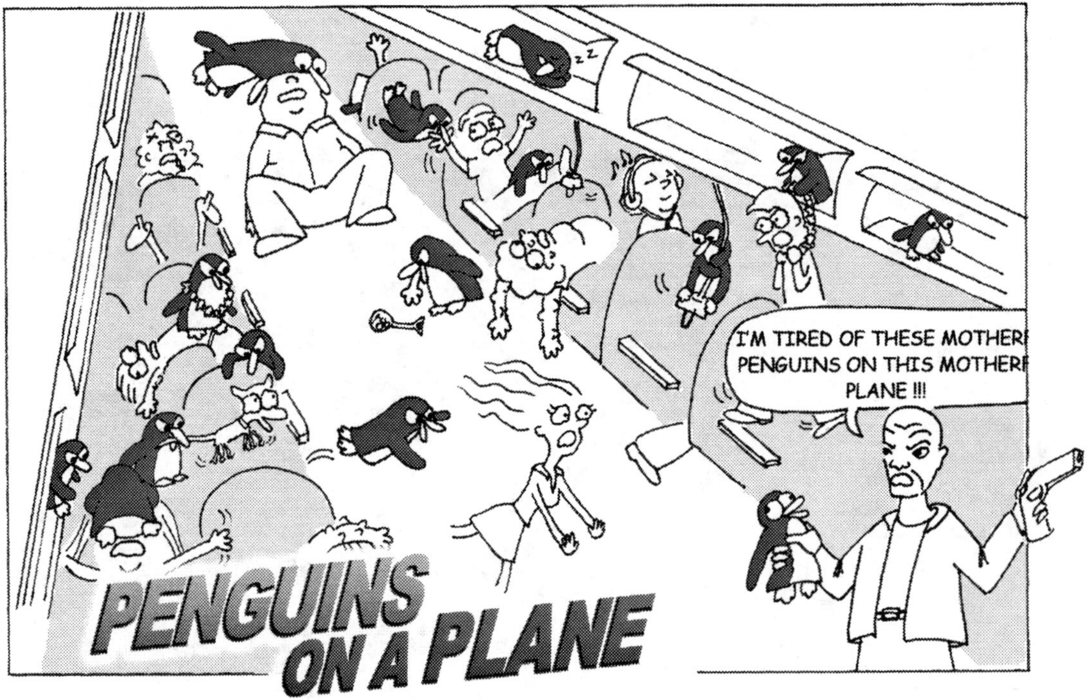

I'M TIRED OF THESE MOTHERF
PENGUINS ON THIS MOTHERF
PLANE !!!
PENGUINS ON A PLANE

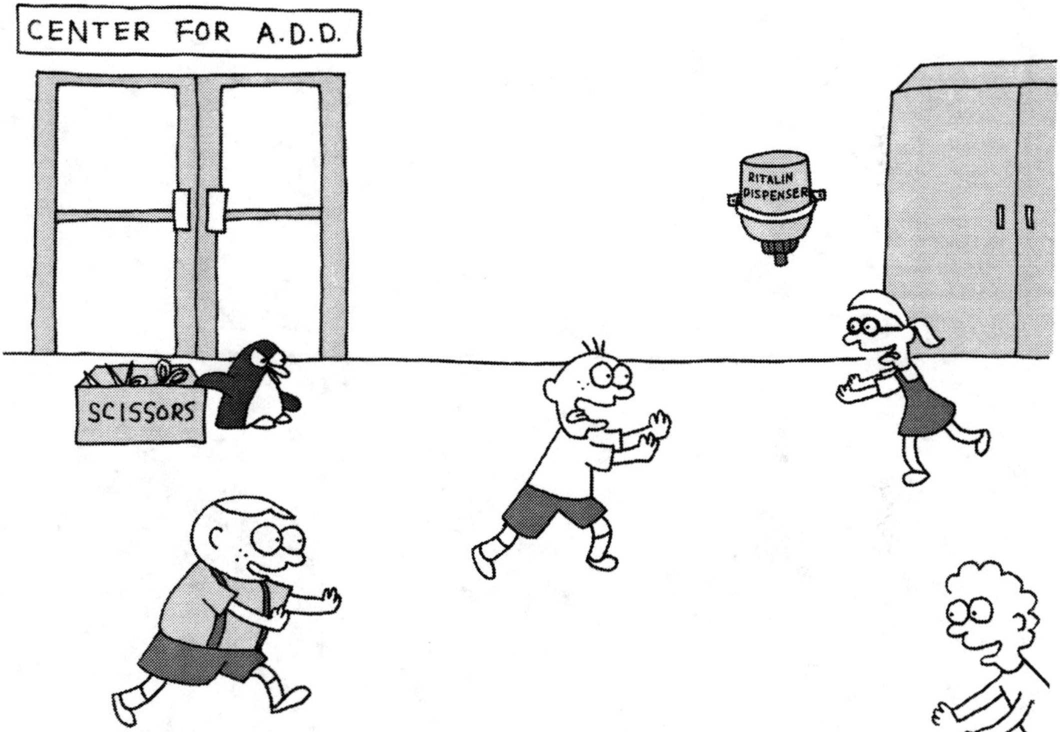
CENTER FOR A.D.D.
RITALIN DISPENSER
SCISSORS

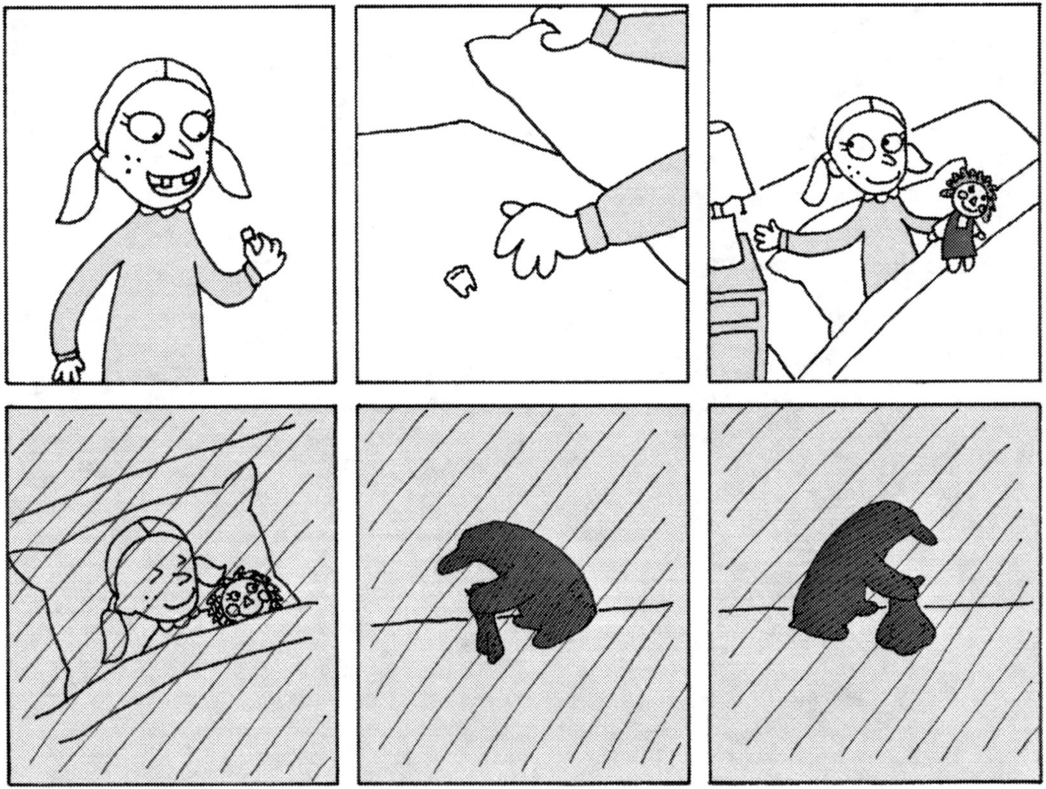

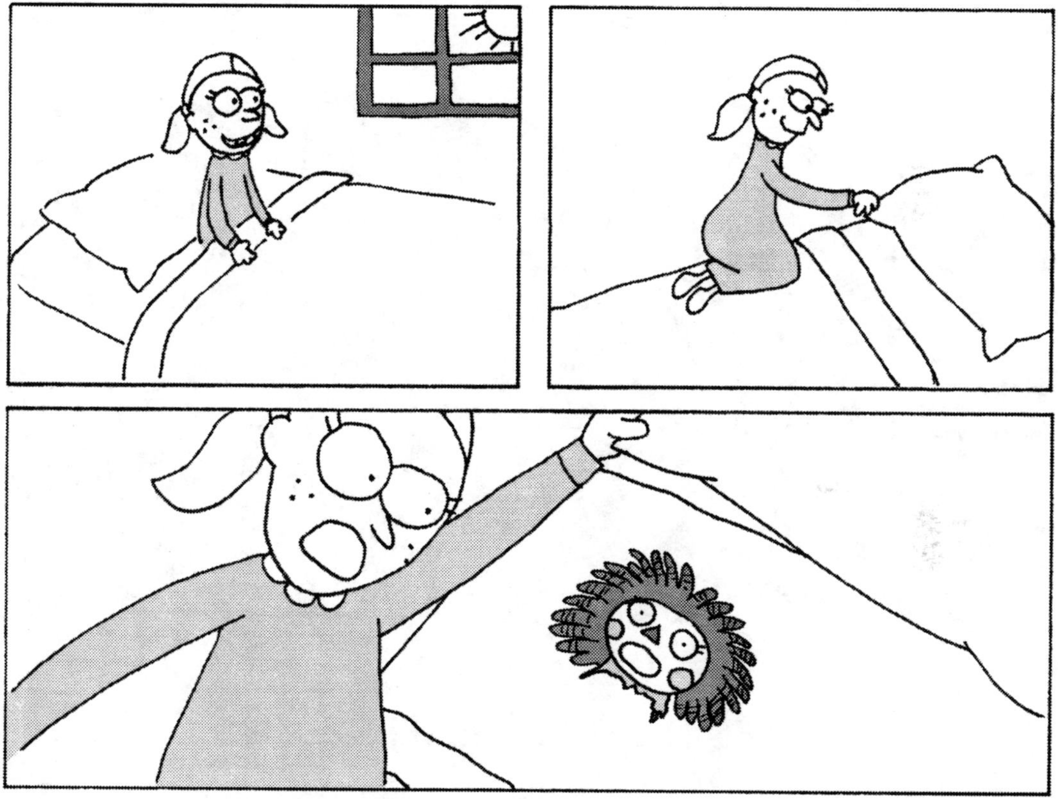

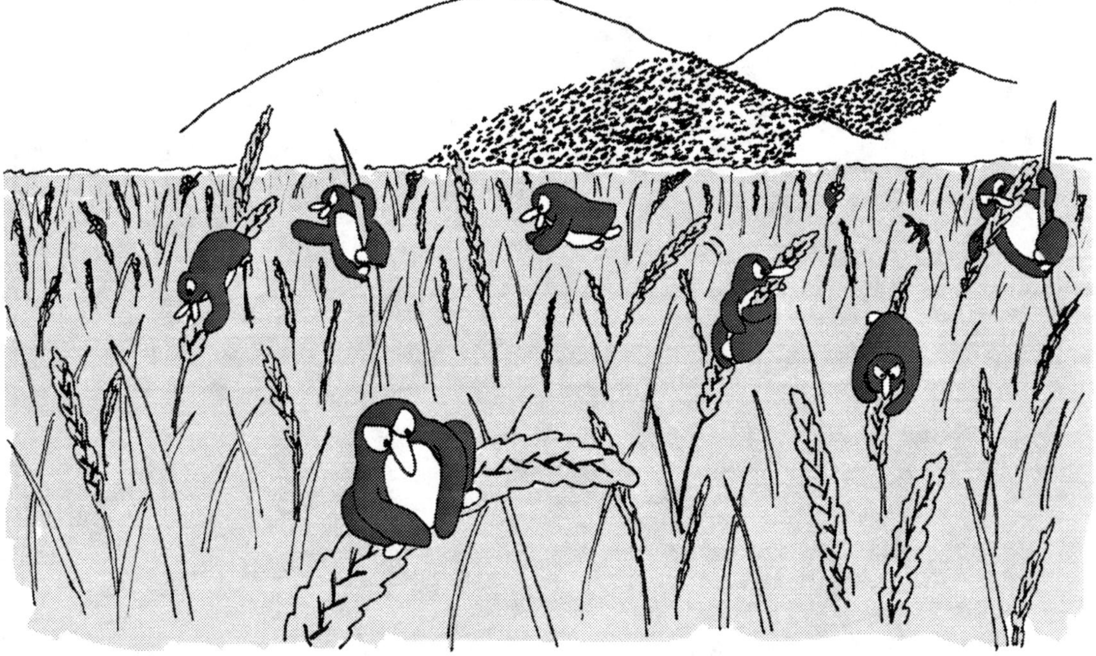

THE 11th PLAGUE: PENGUINS

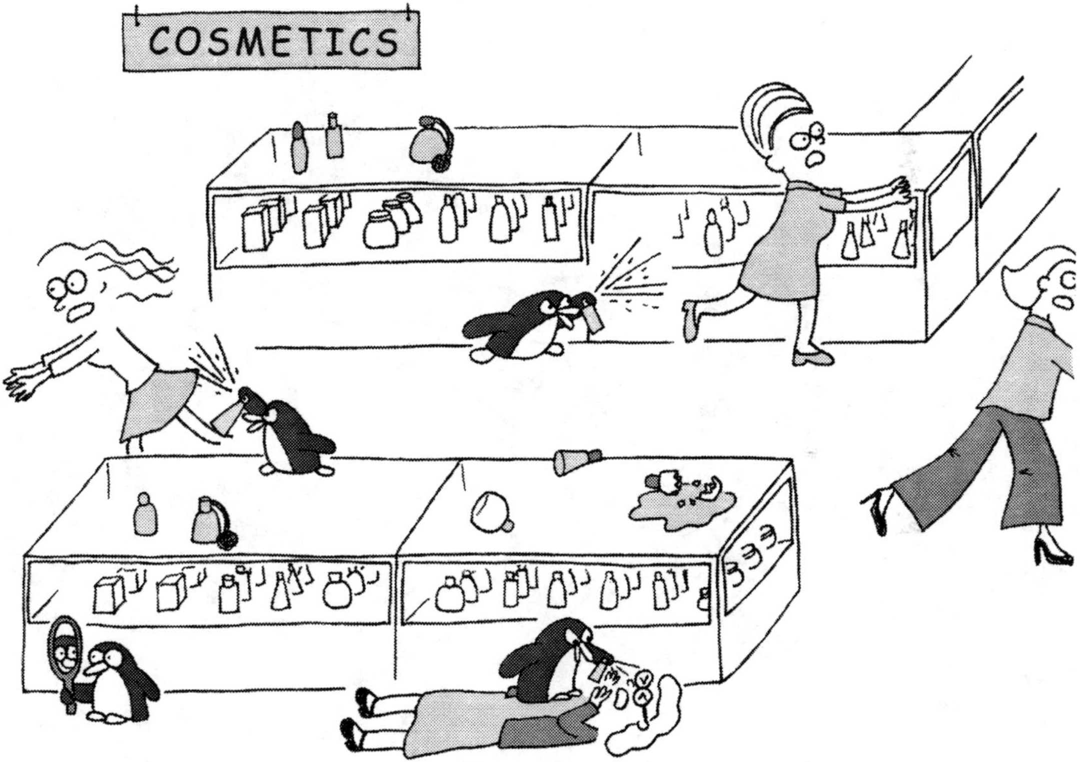
COSMETICS

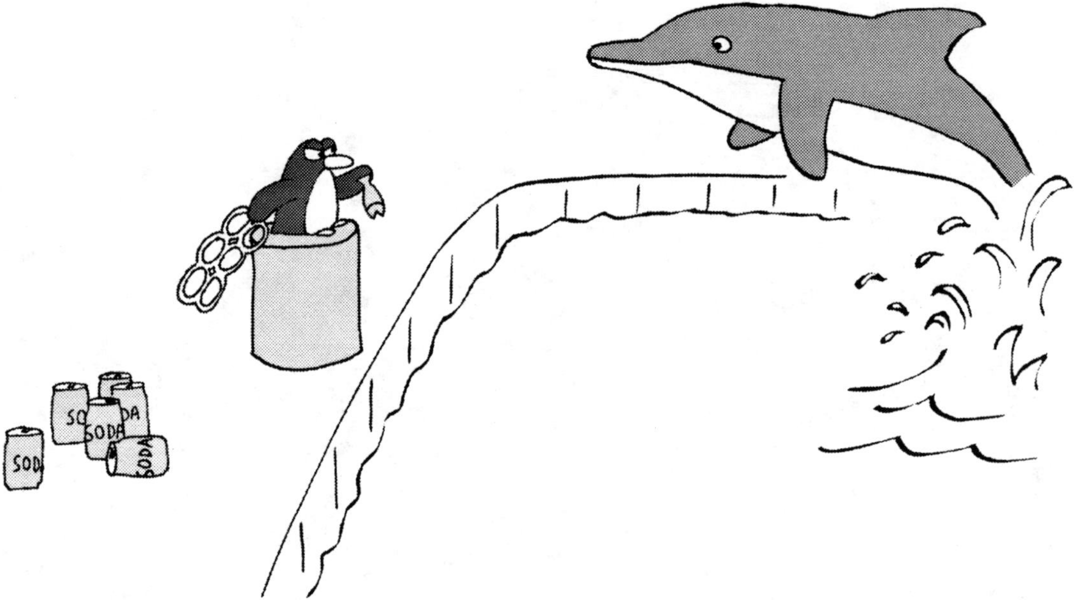

SODA
SODA
SODA
SODA

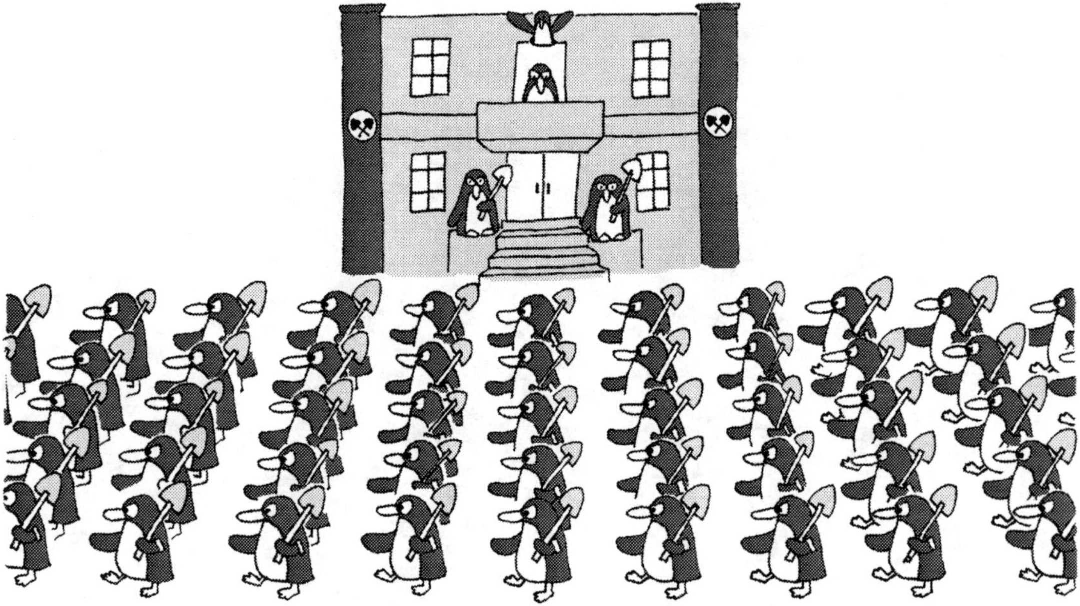

MARCH OF THE PENGUINS

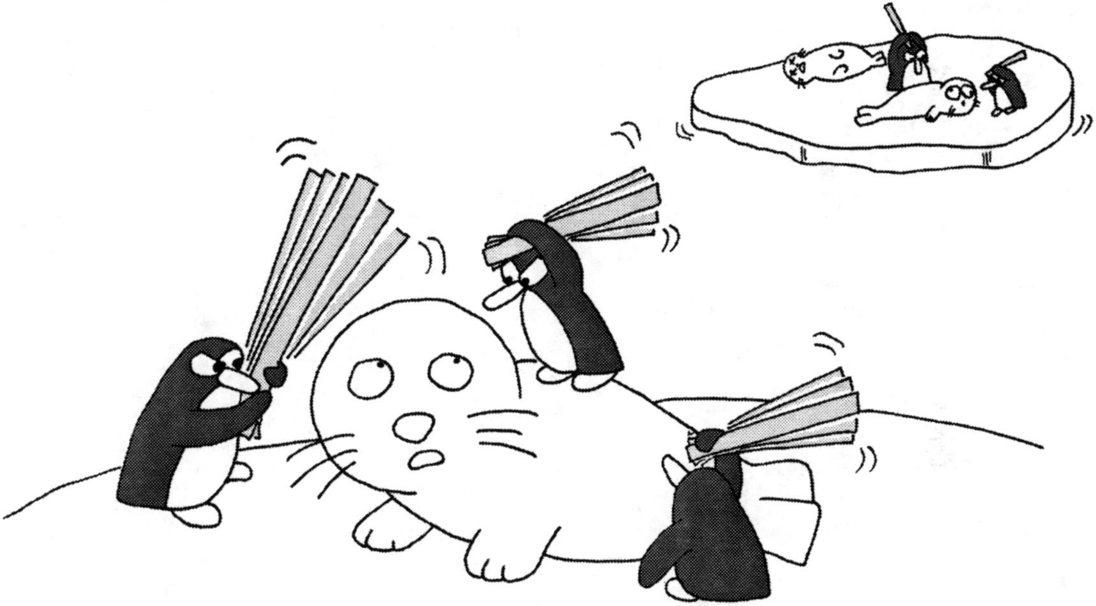

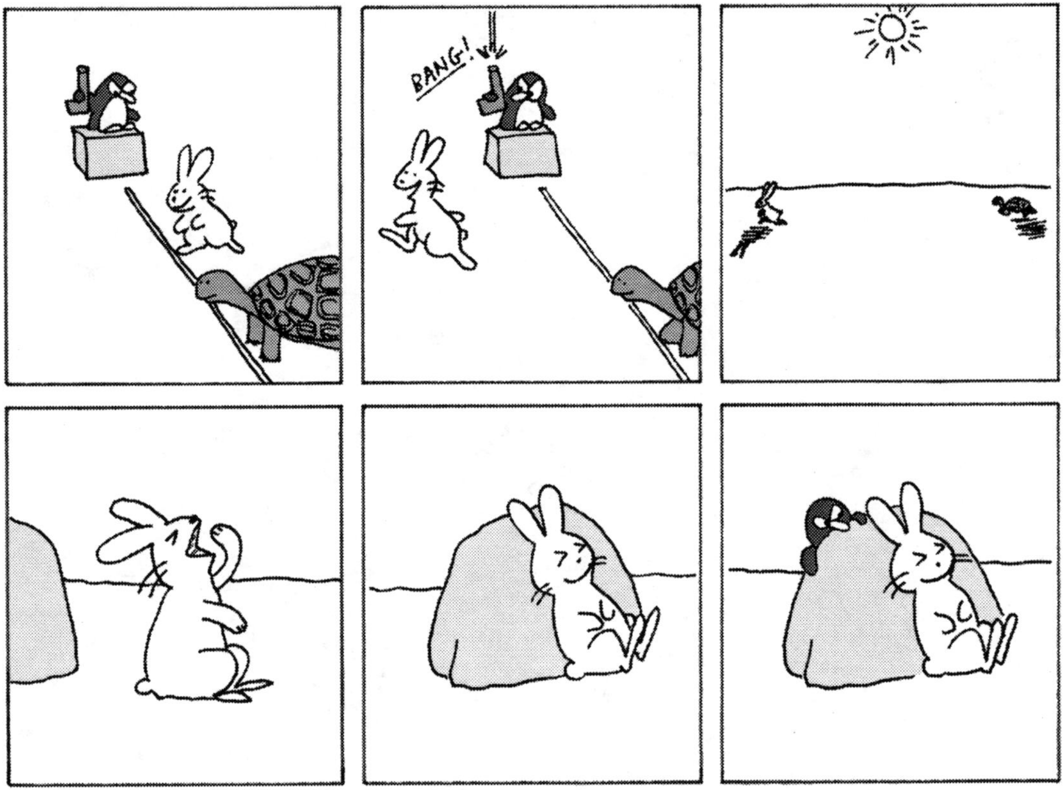
BANG!

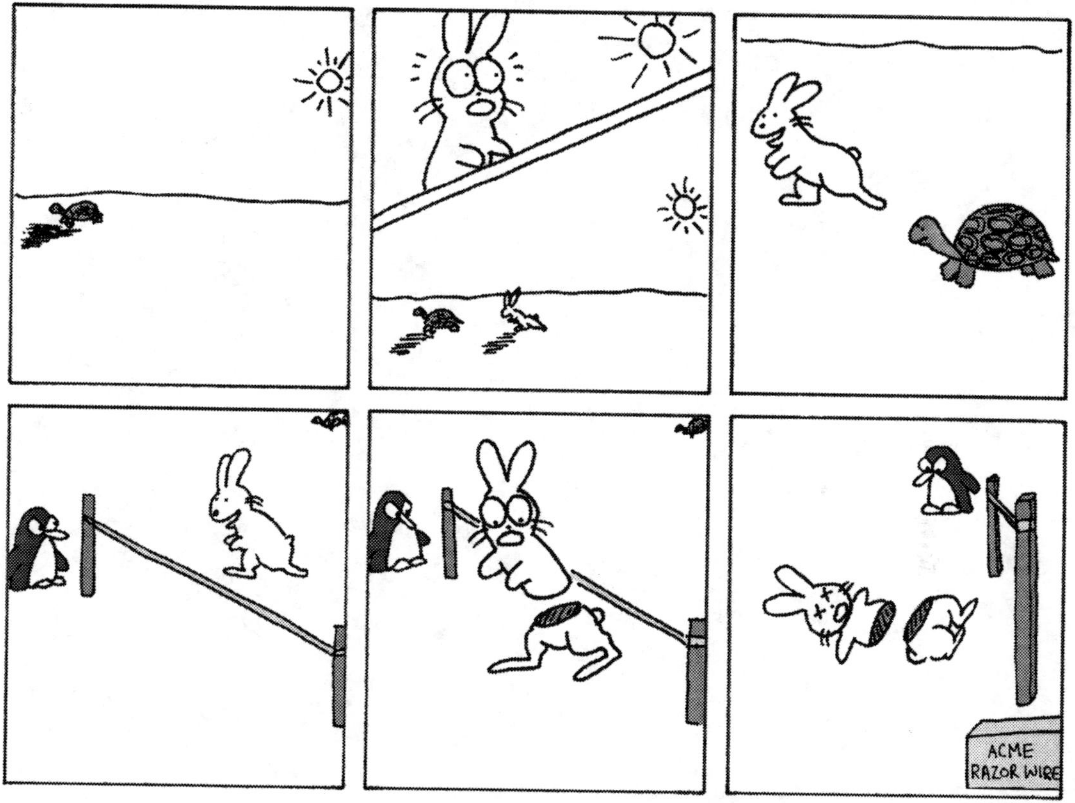
ACME
RAZOR WIRE

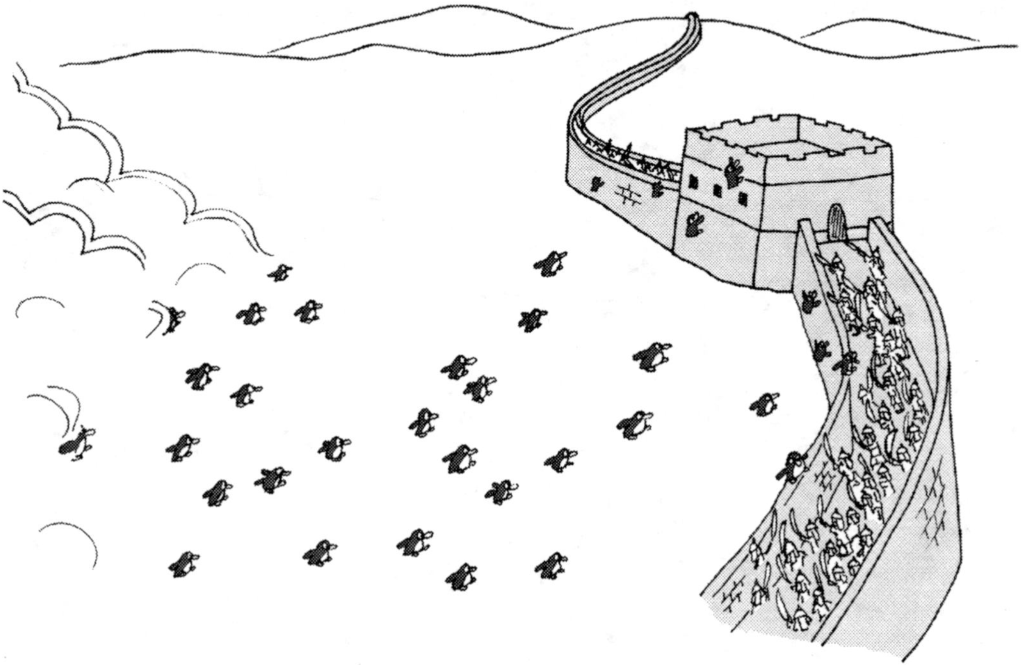

The Chinese Empire defends against the barbarian hordes from Antarctica.

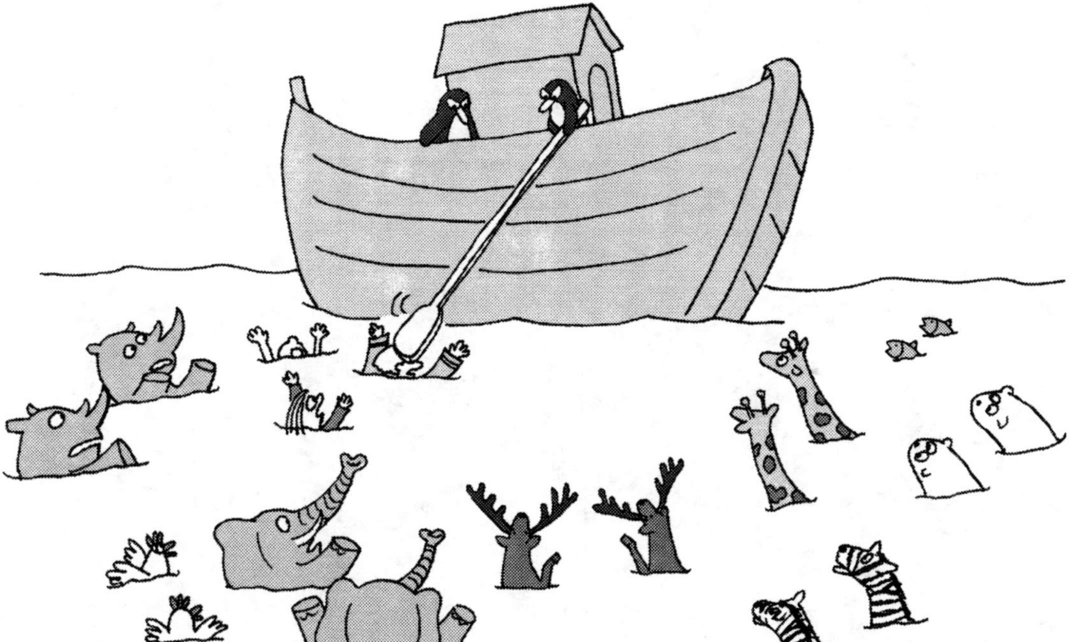

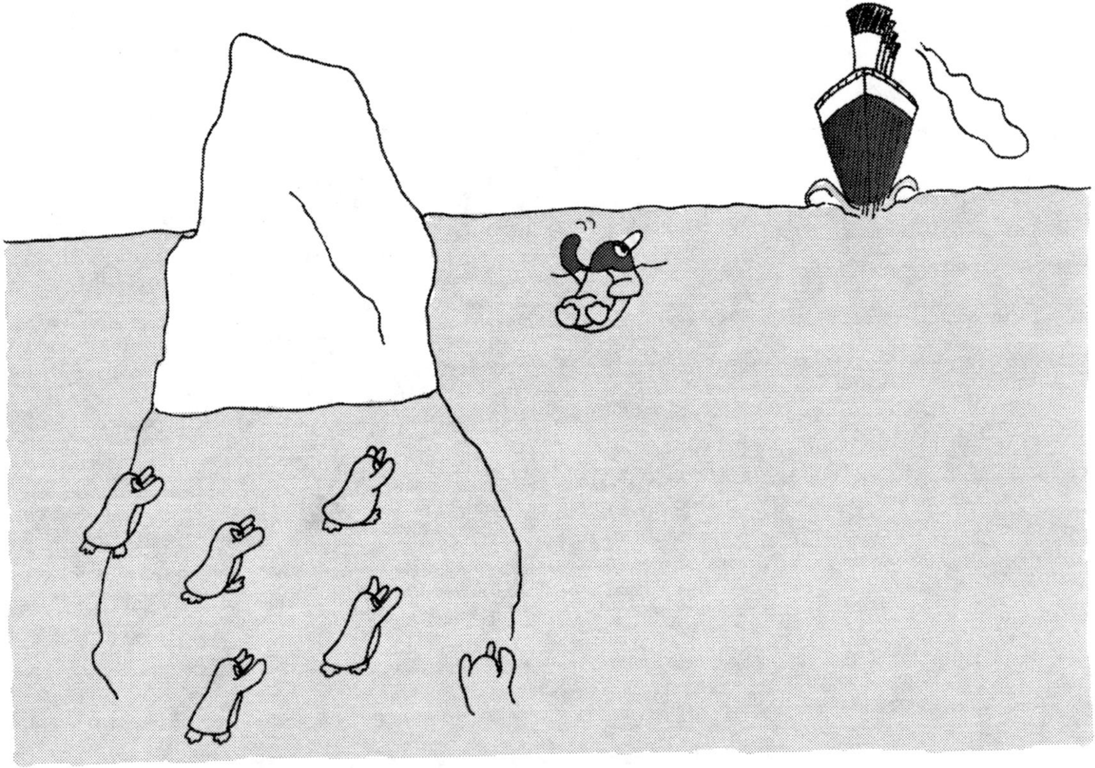

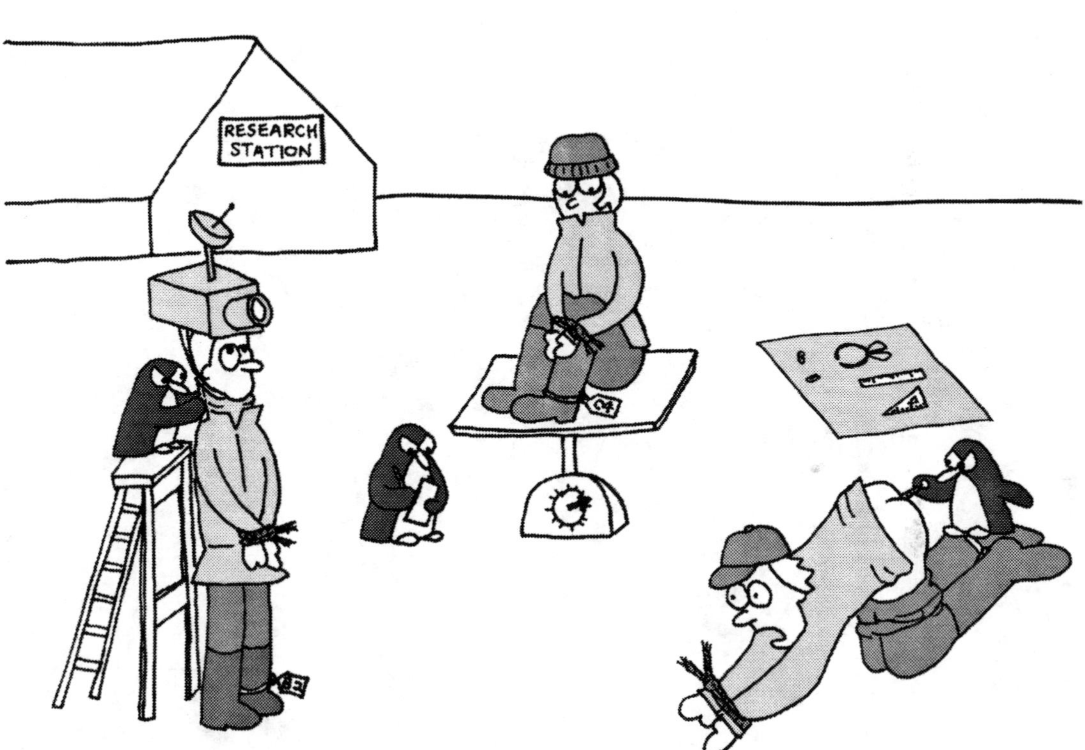
RESEARCH
STATION

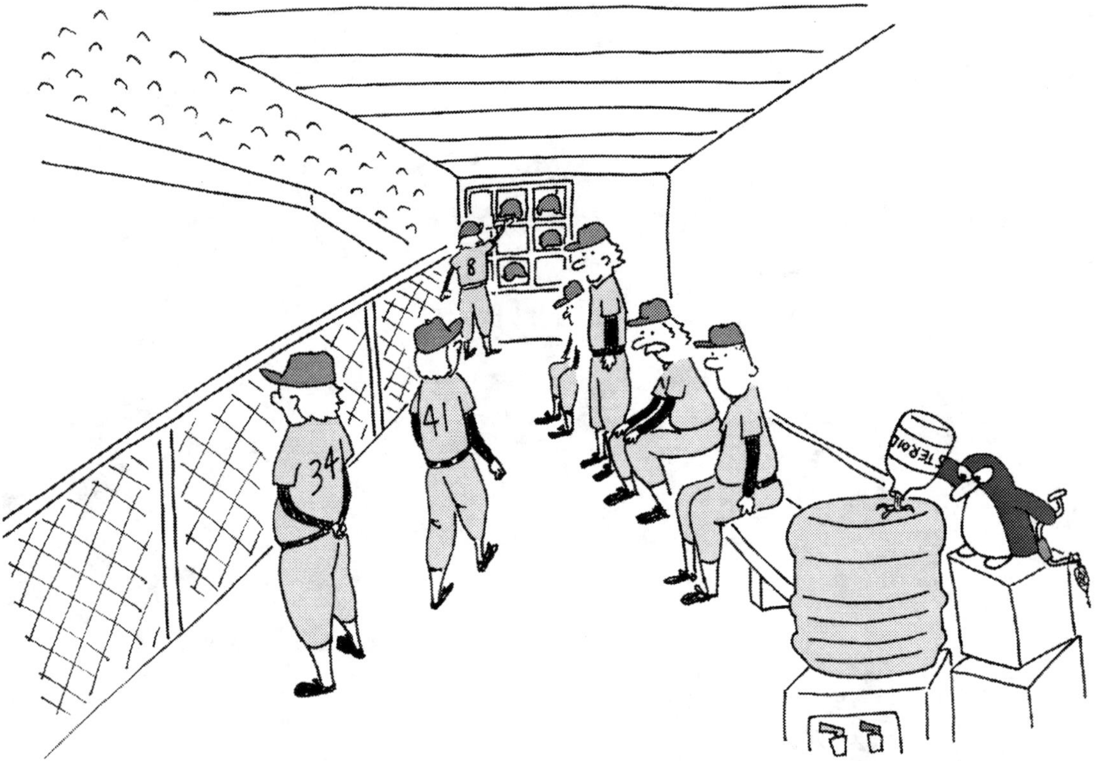
8
41
34
TEROID

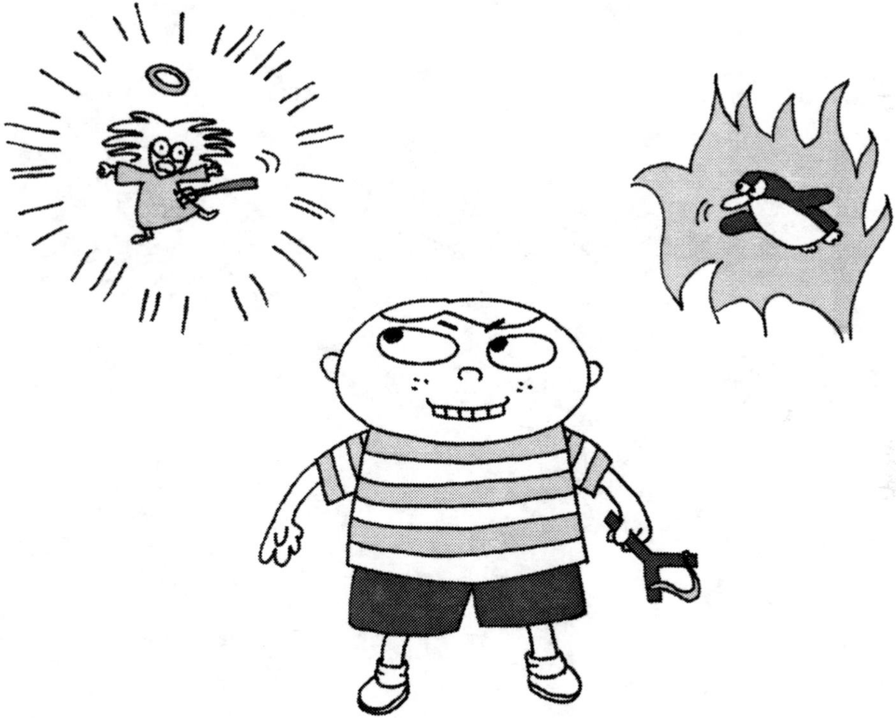

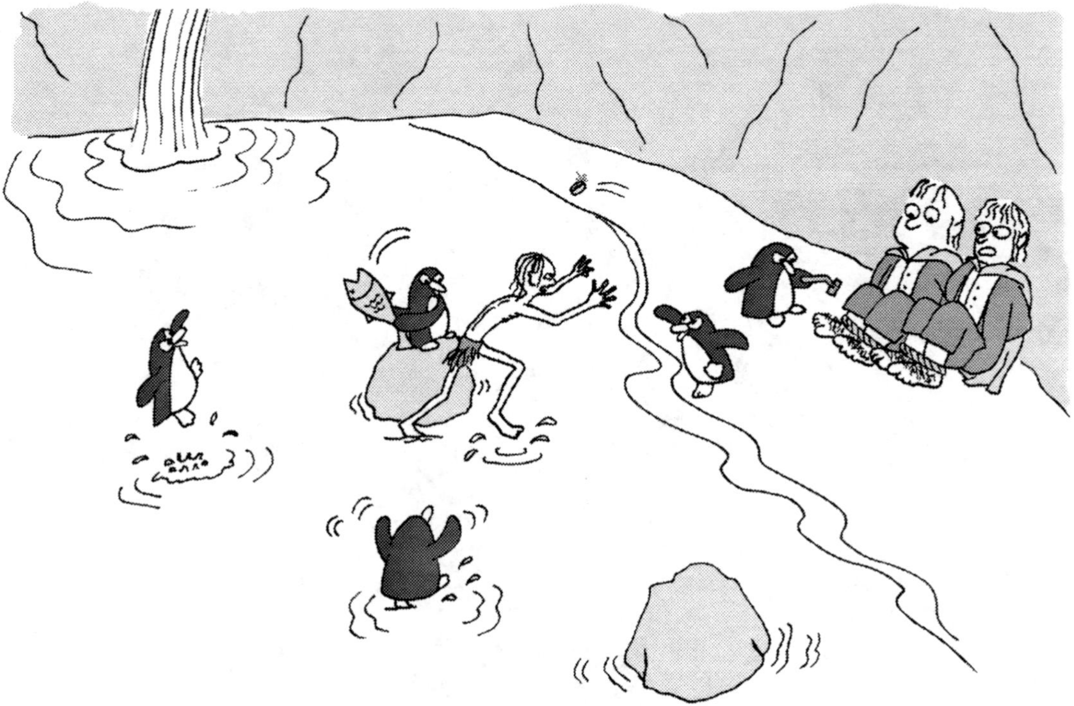

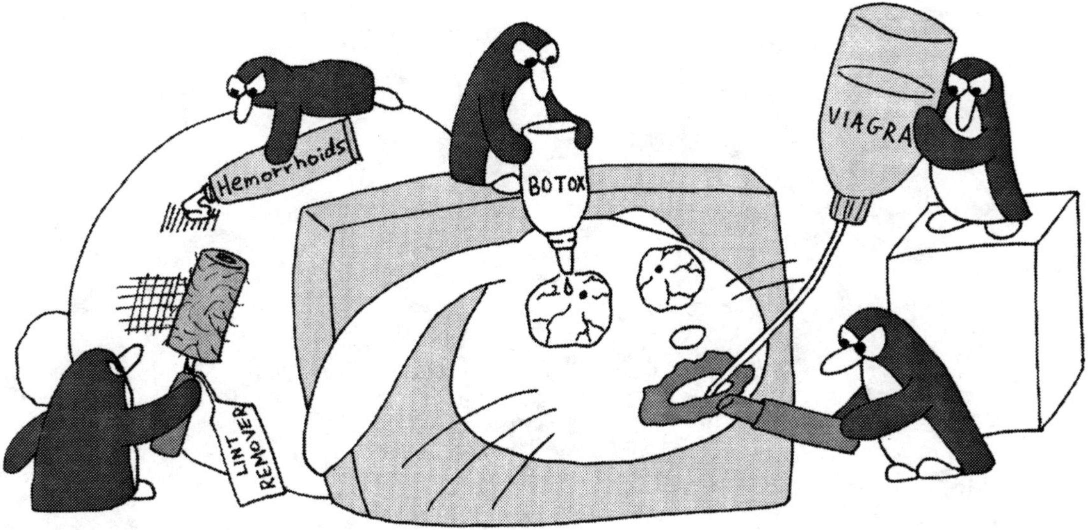
Hemorrhoids
BOTOX
VIAGRA
LINT REMOVER

ANIMAL TESTING

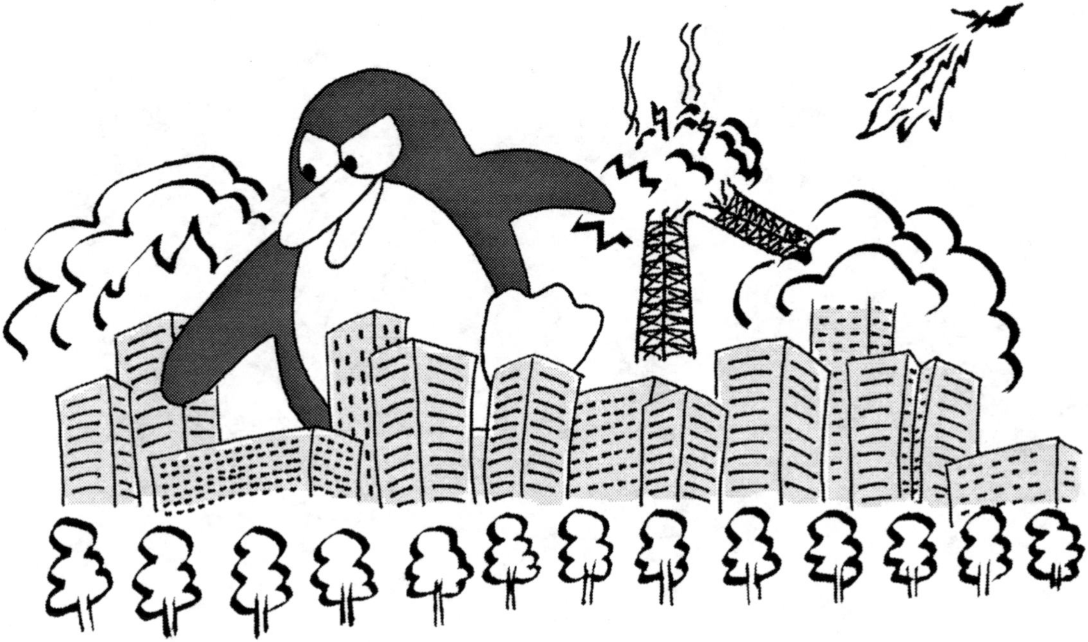

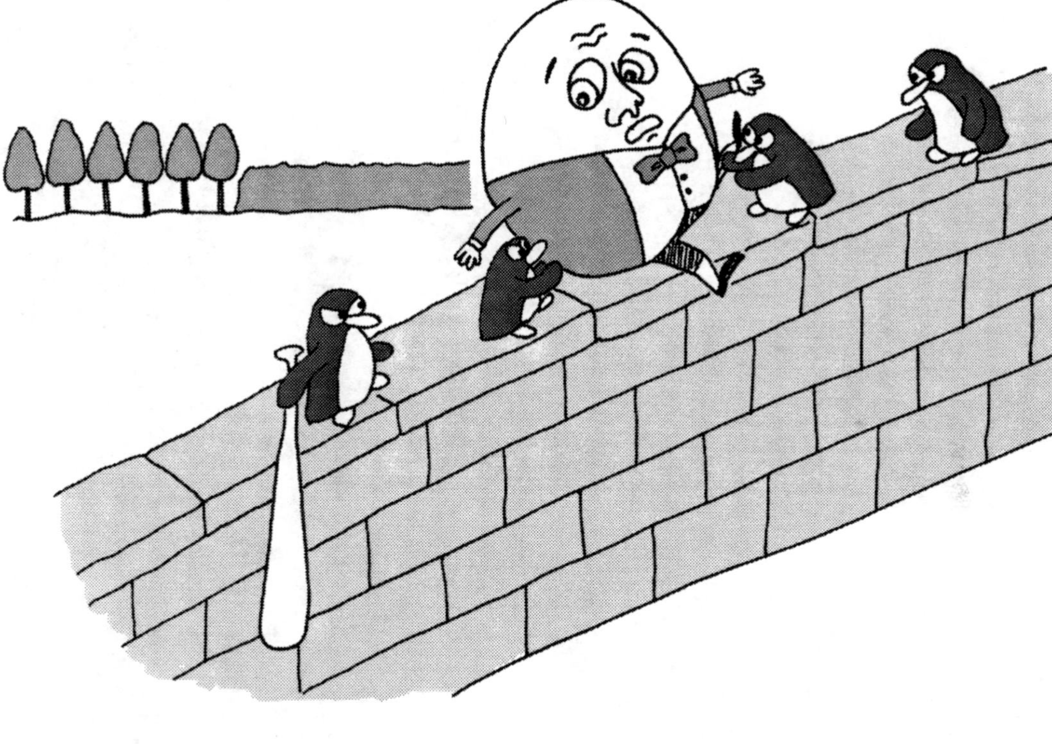

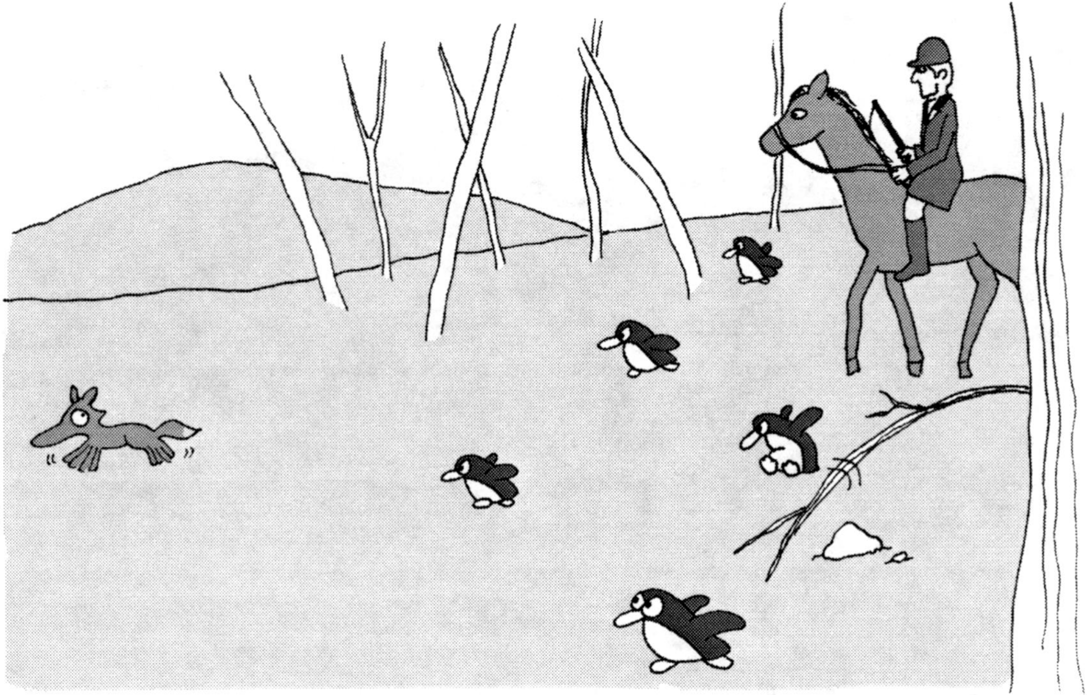

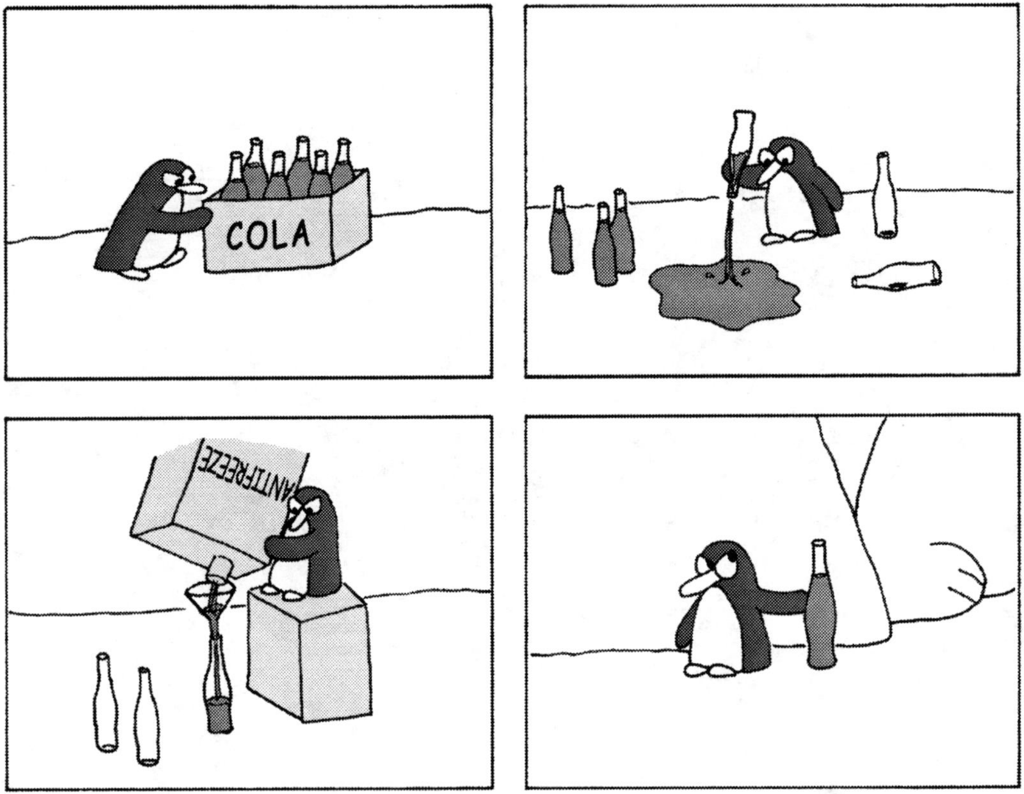
COLA
ANTIFREEZE

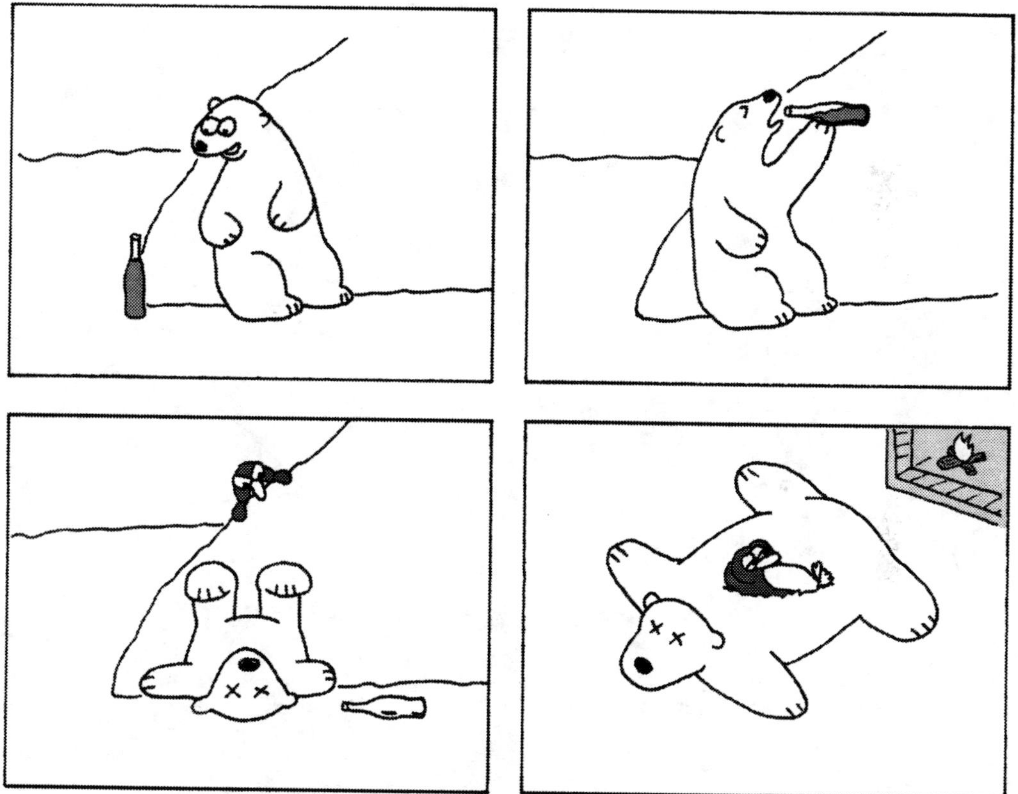

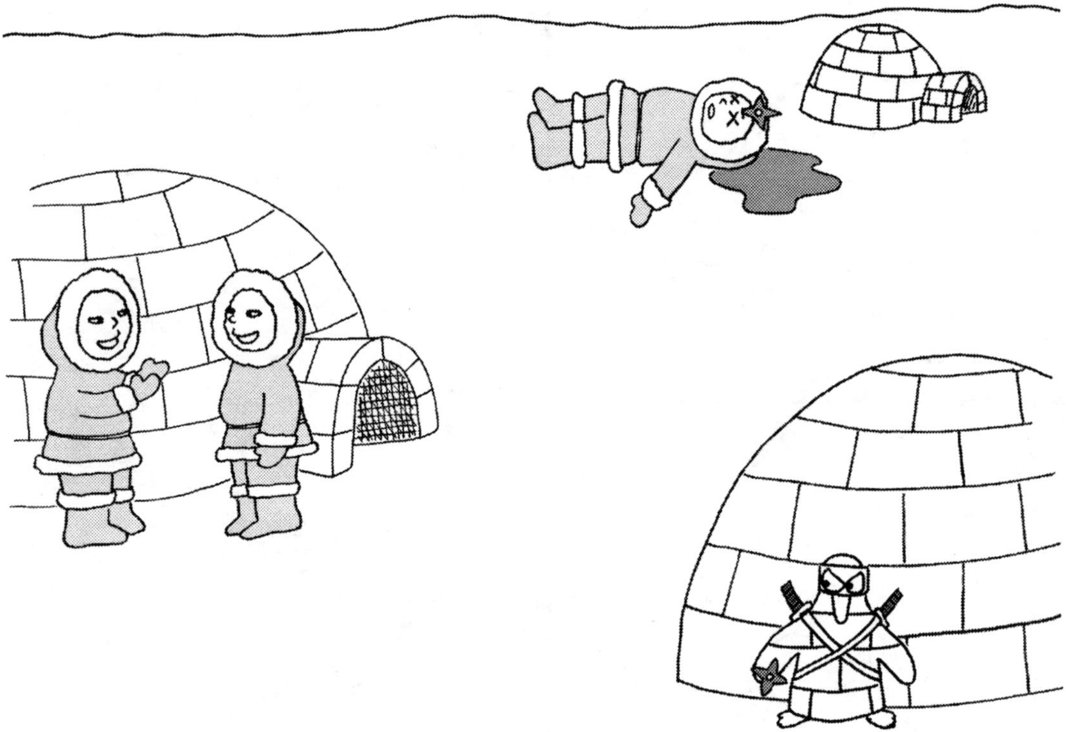

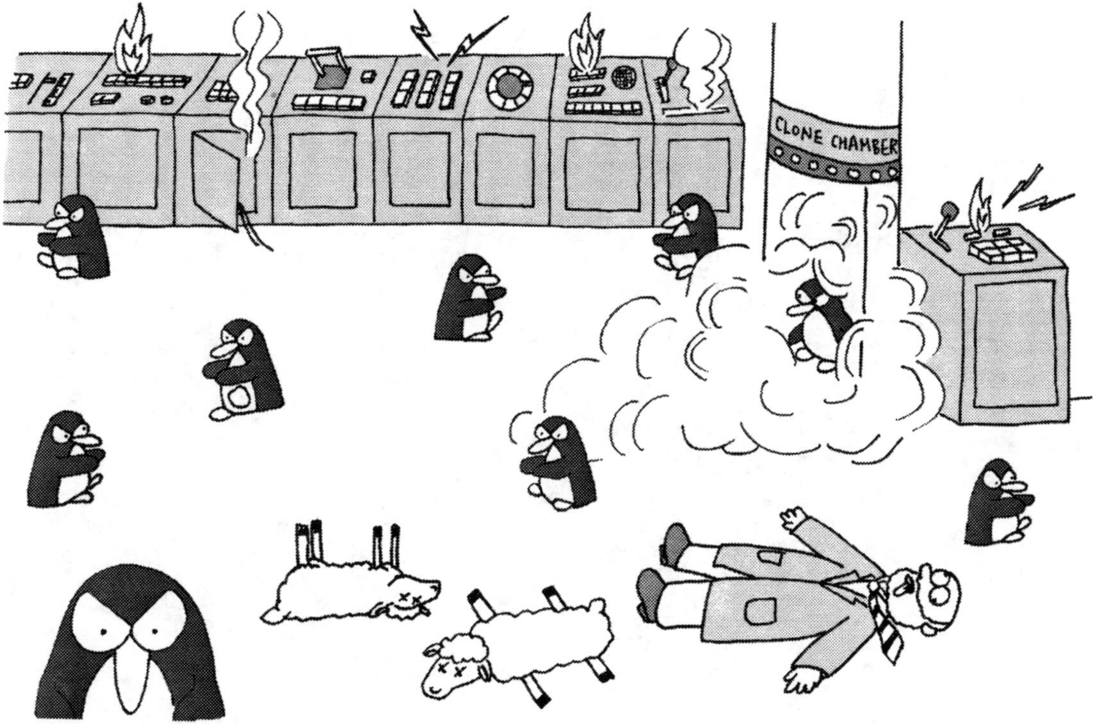
CLONE CHAMBER

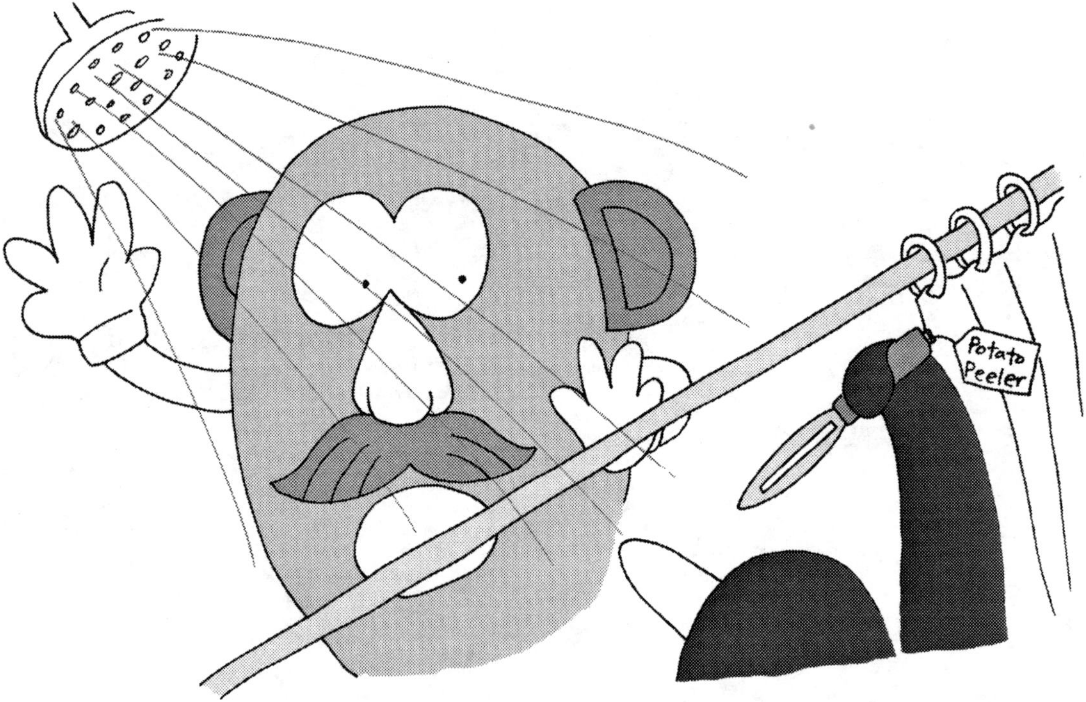
Potato Peeler

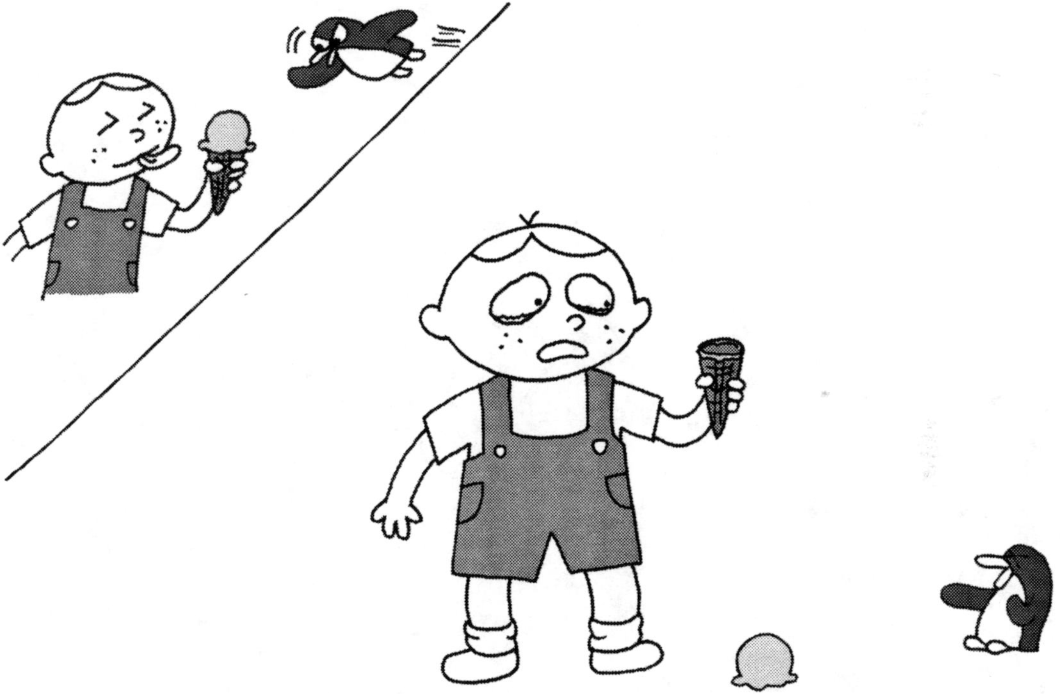

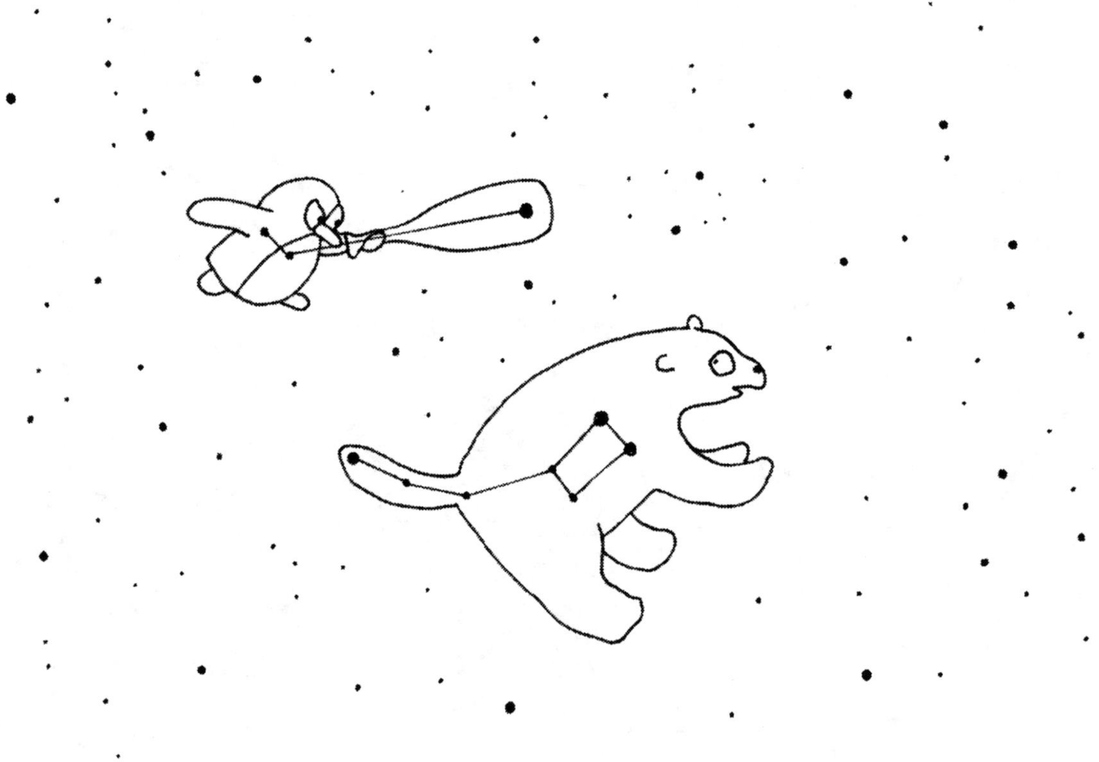

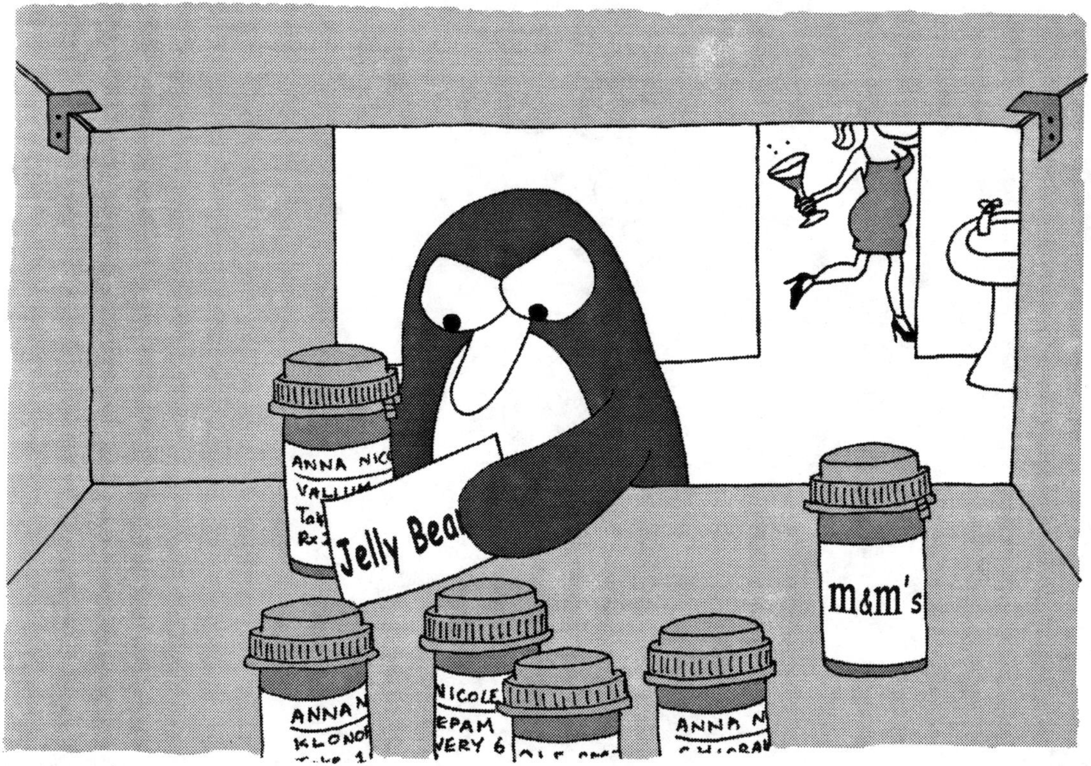
ANNA
m&m's

D E A D

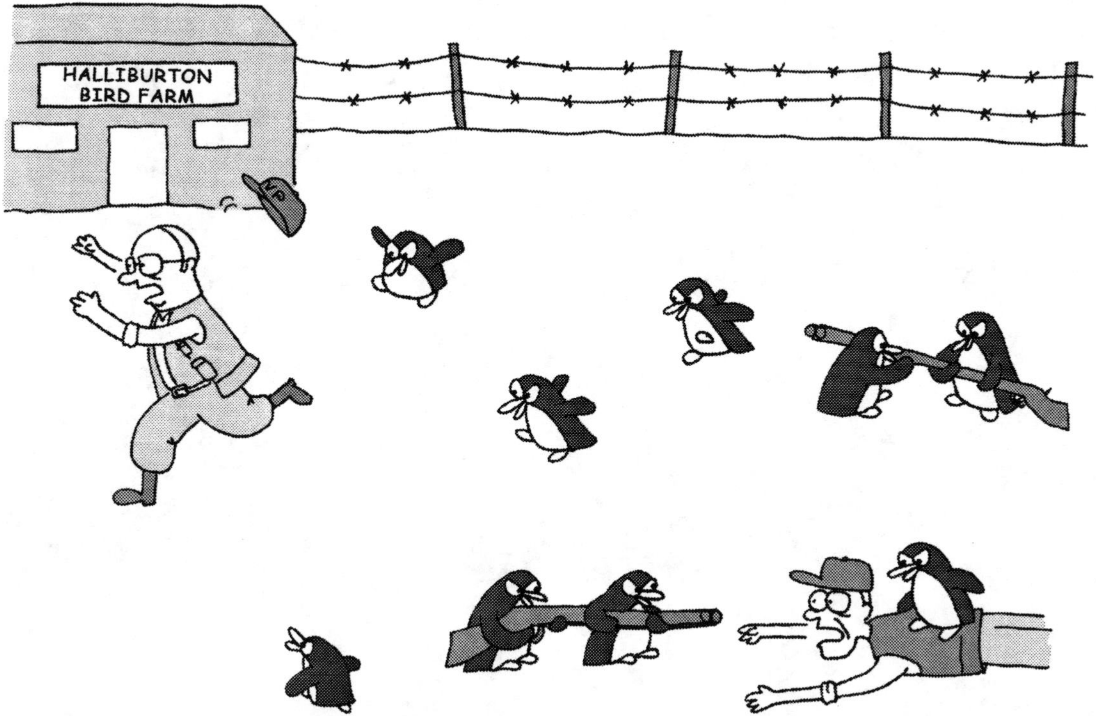
HALLIBURTON
BIRD FARM
VP

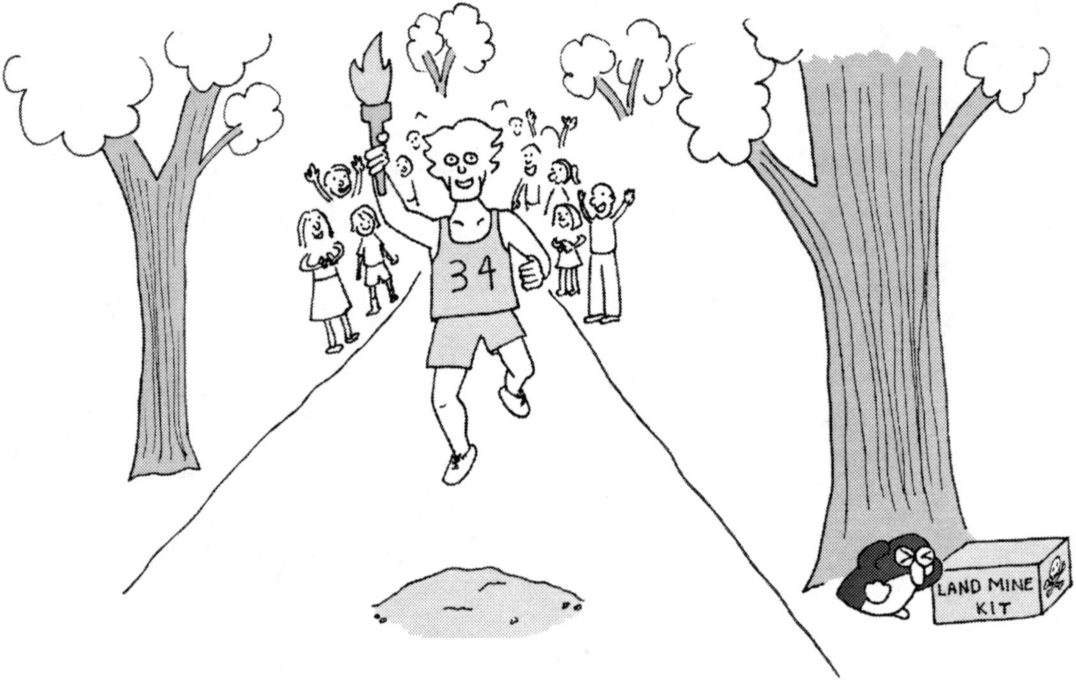
34
LAND MINE
KIT

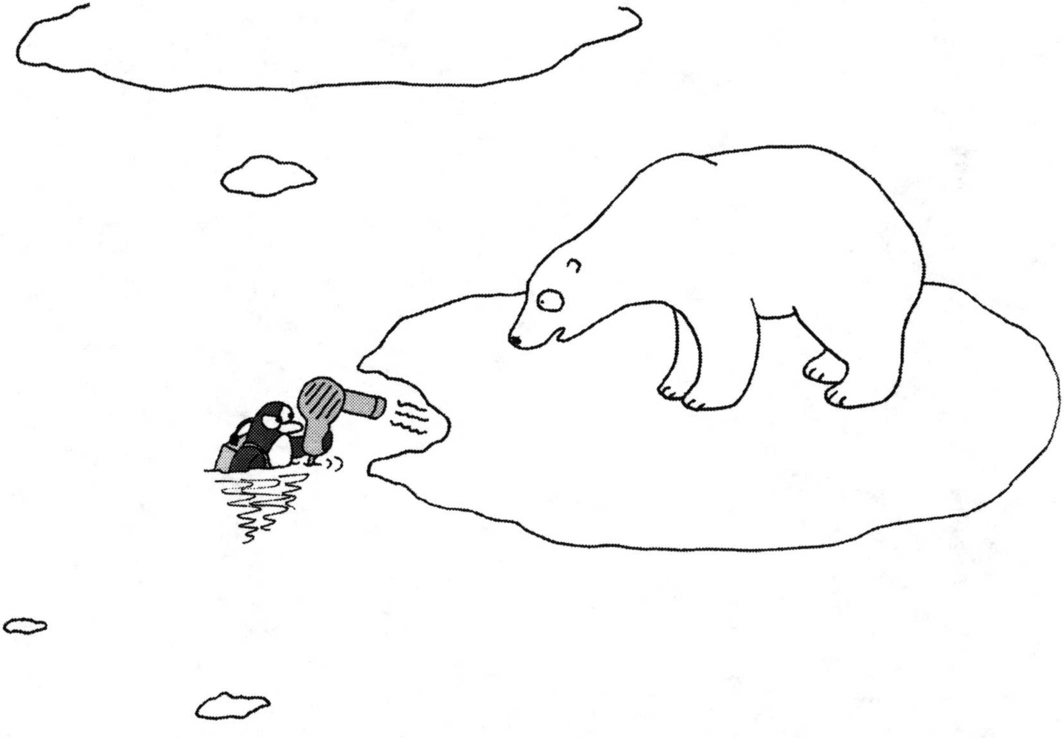

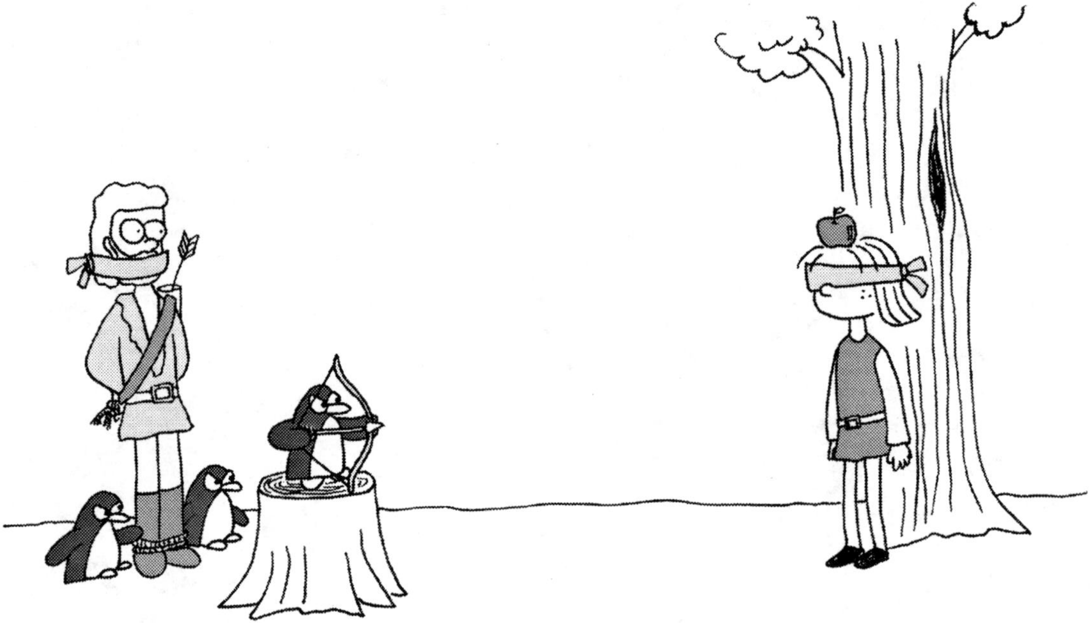

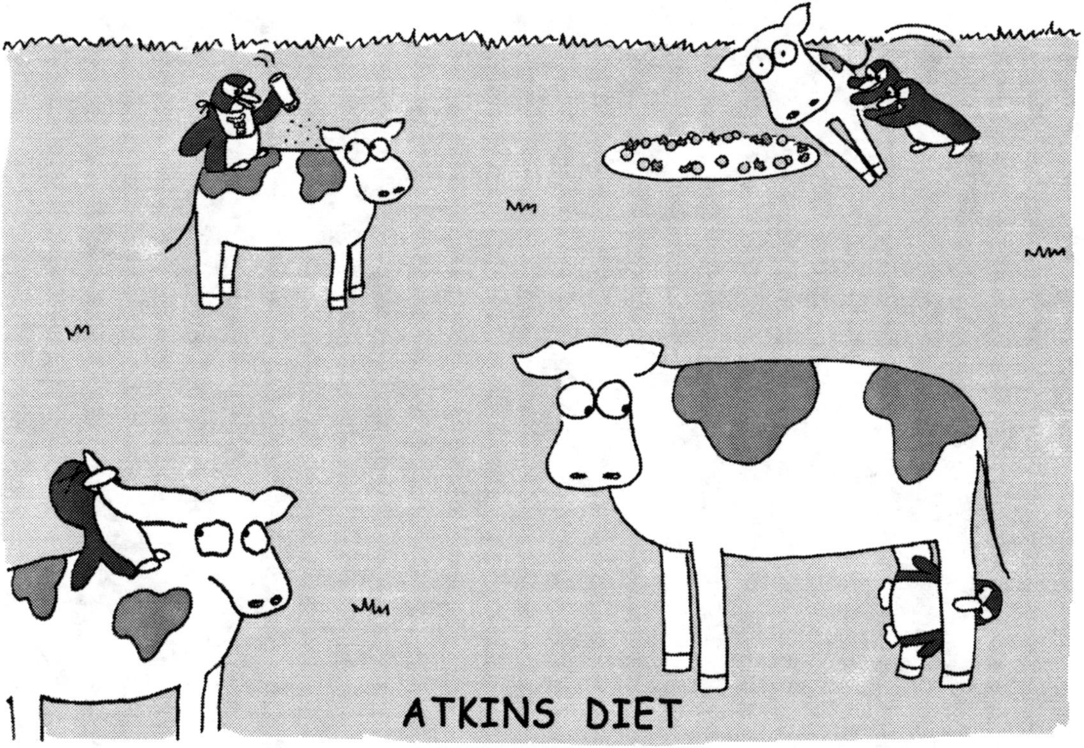

ATKINS DIET

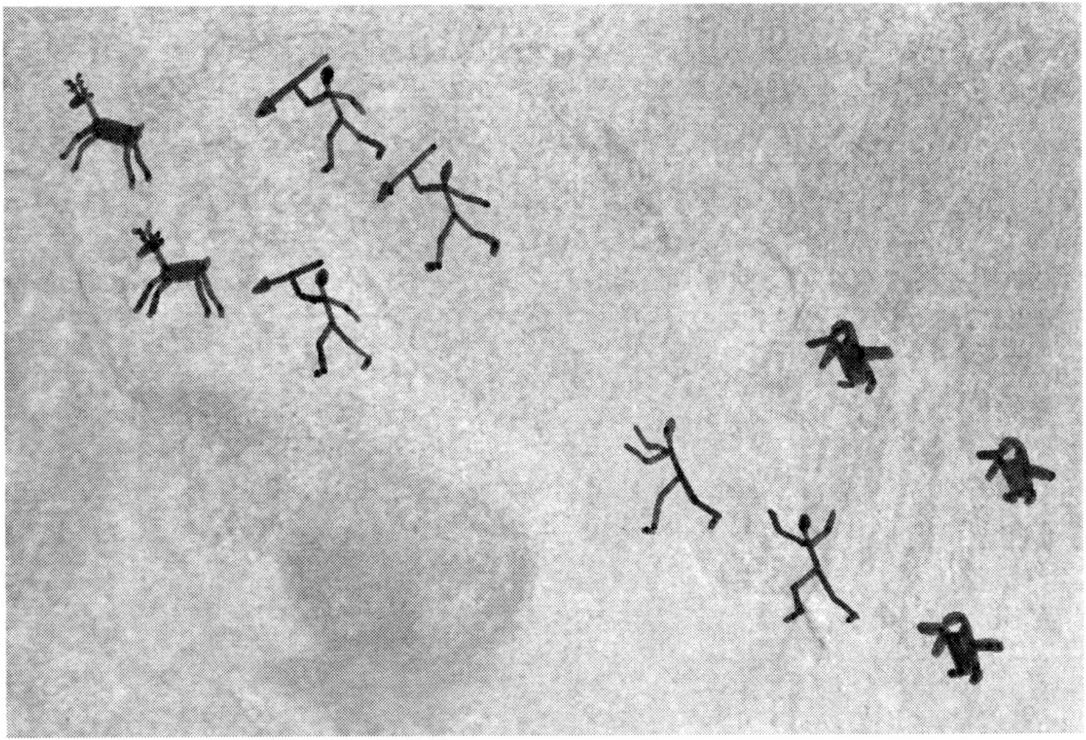

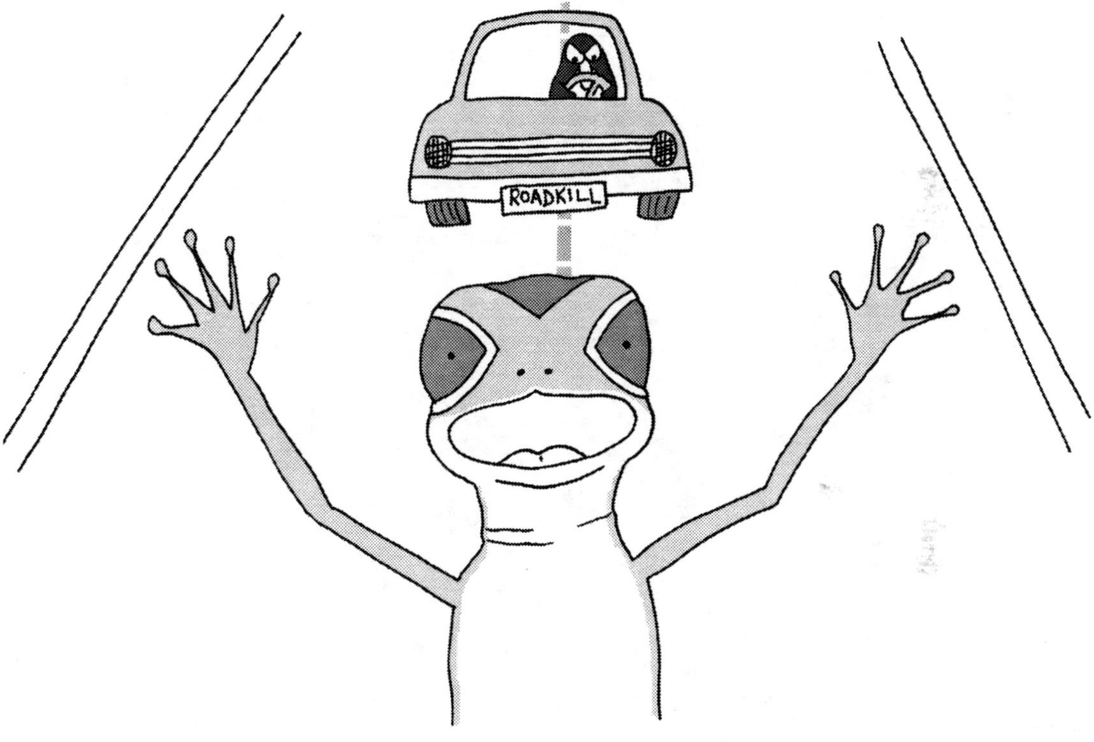
ROADKILL

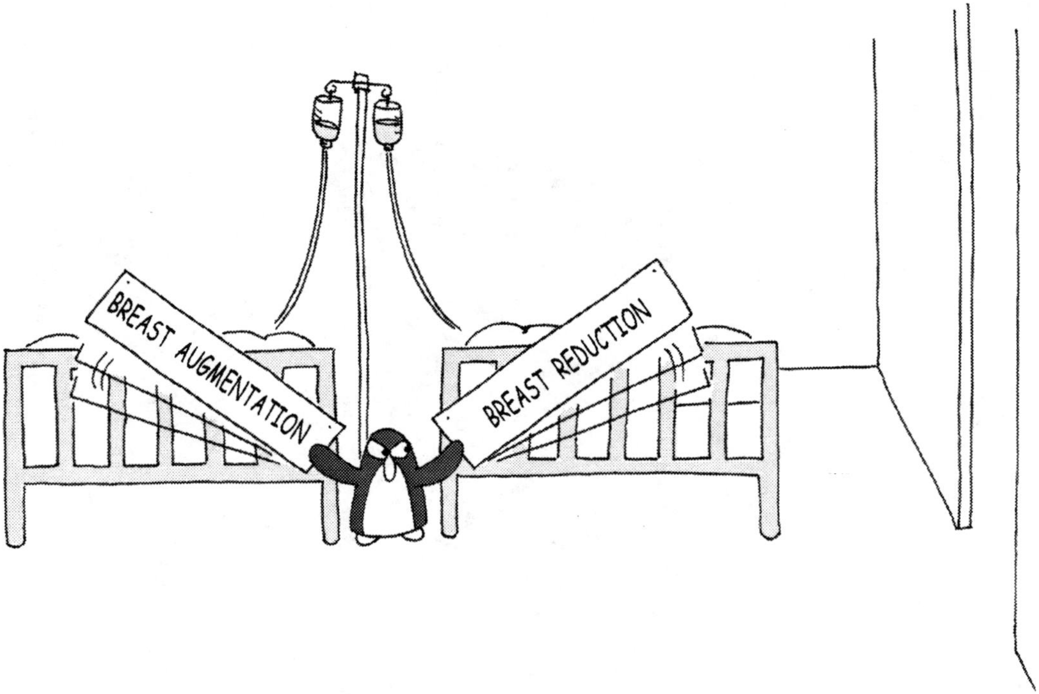
BREAST AUGMENTATION
BREAST REDUCTION

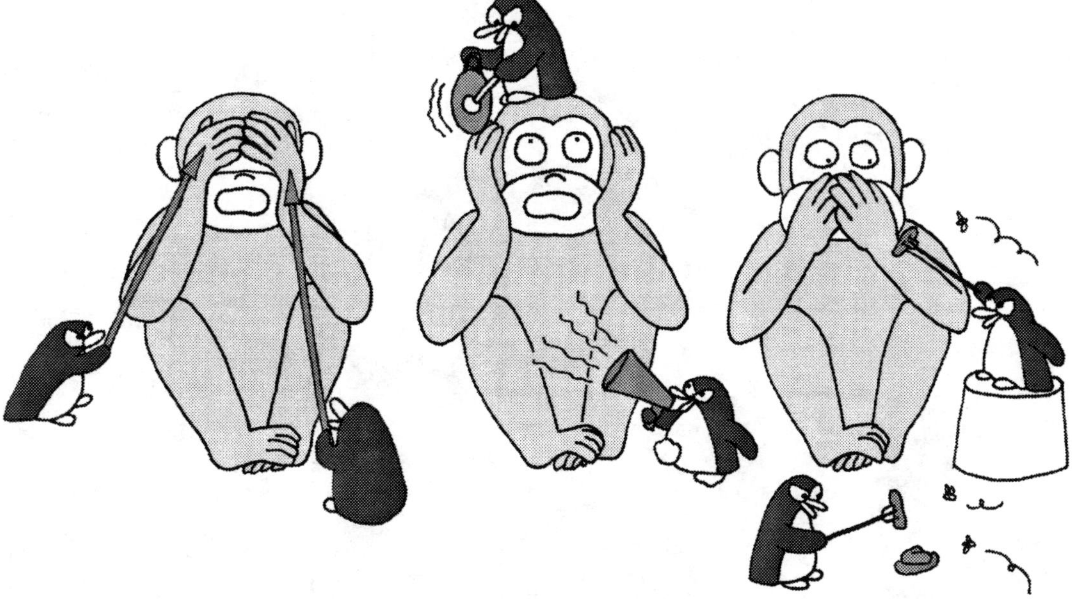

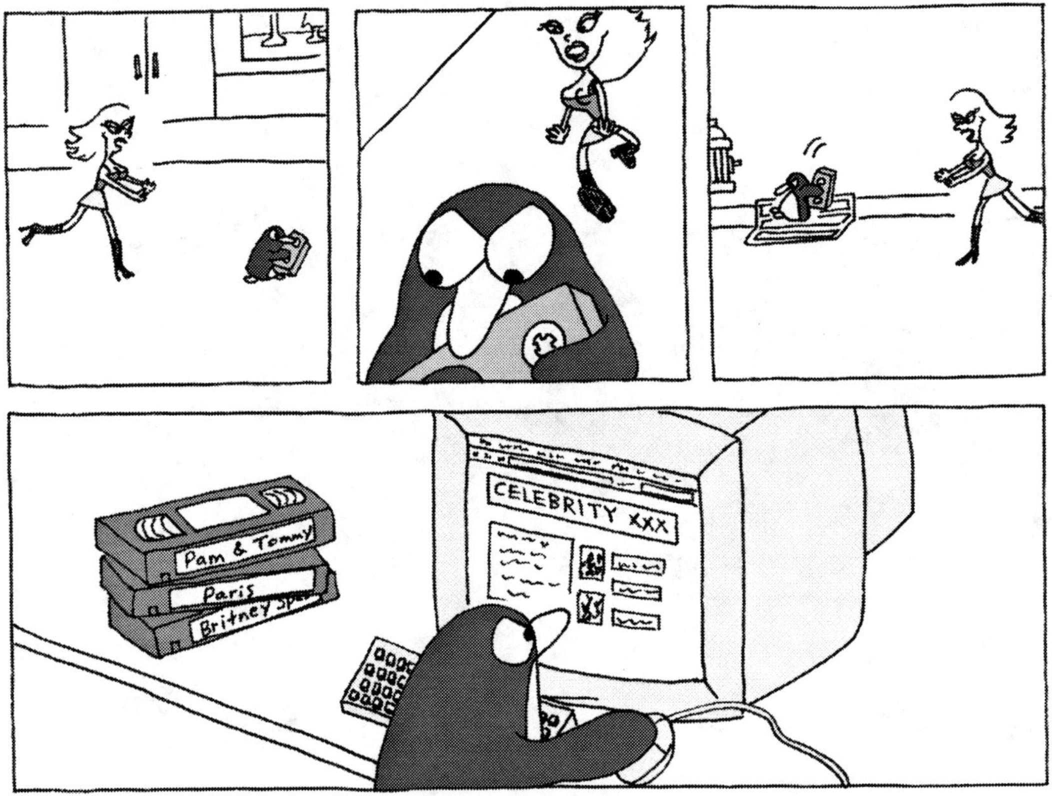
CELEBRITY XXX
Pam & Tommy
Paris
Britney

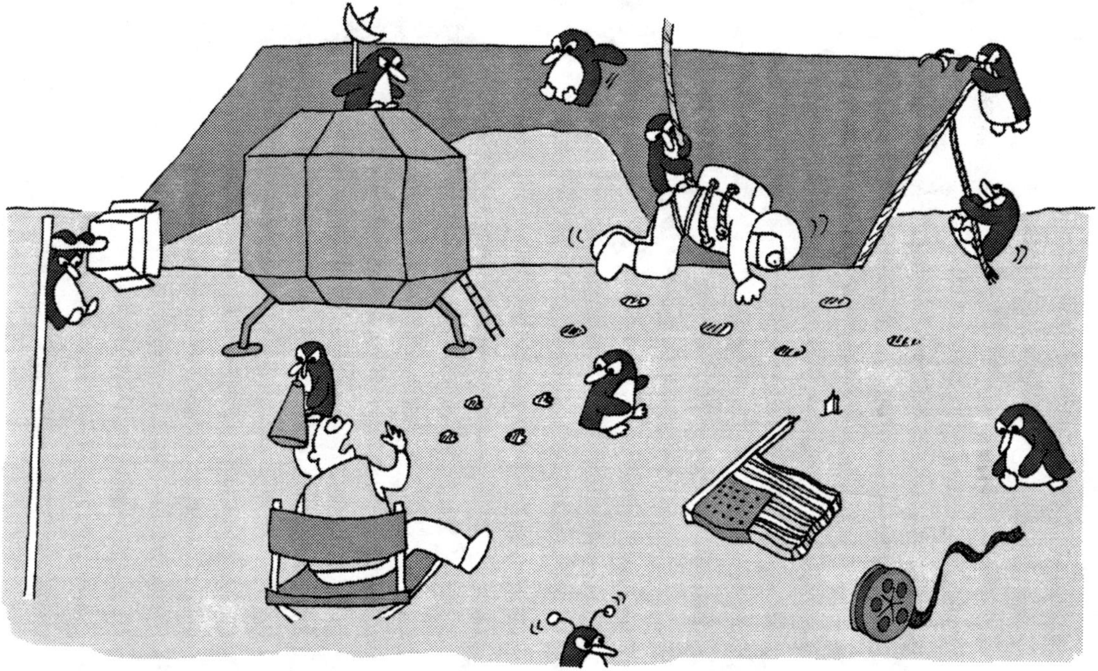

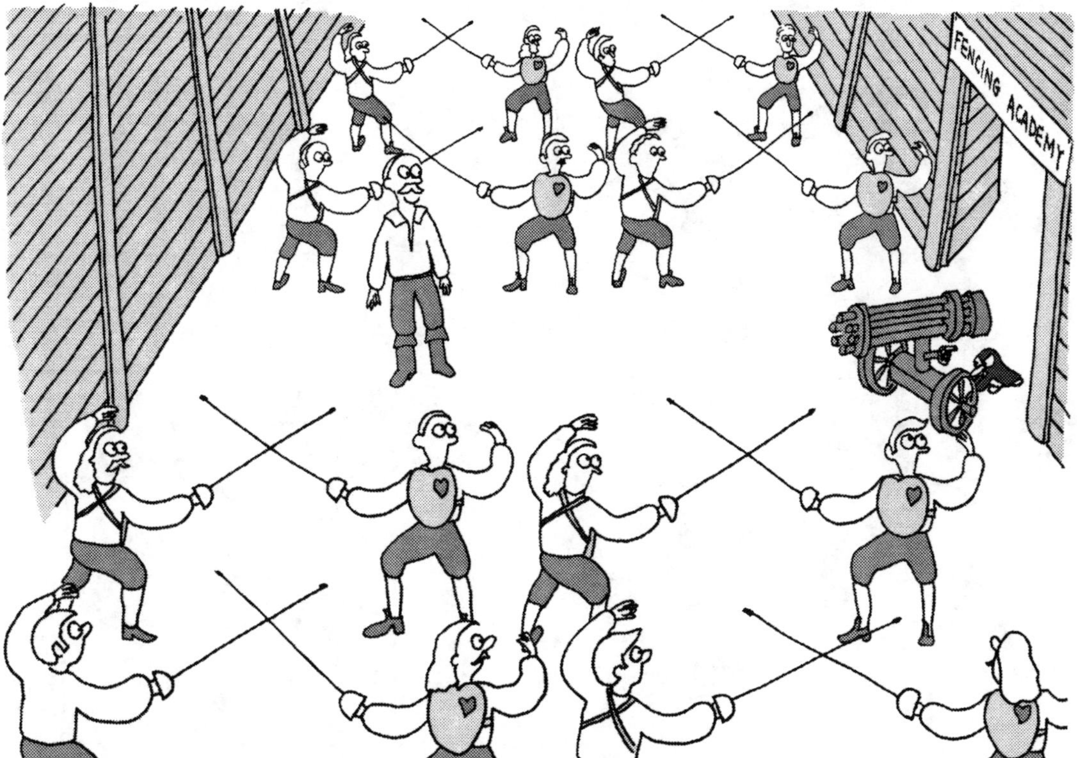
FENCING ACADEMY

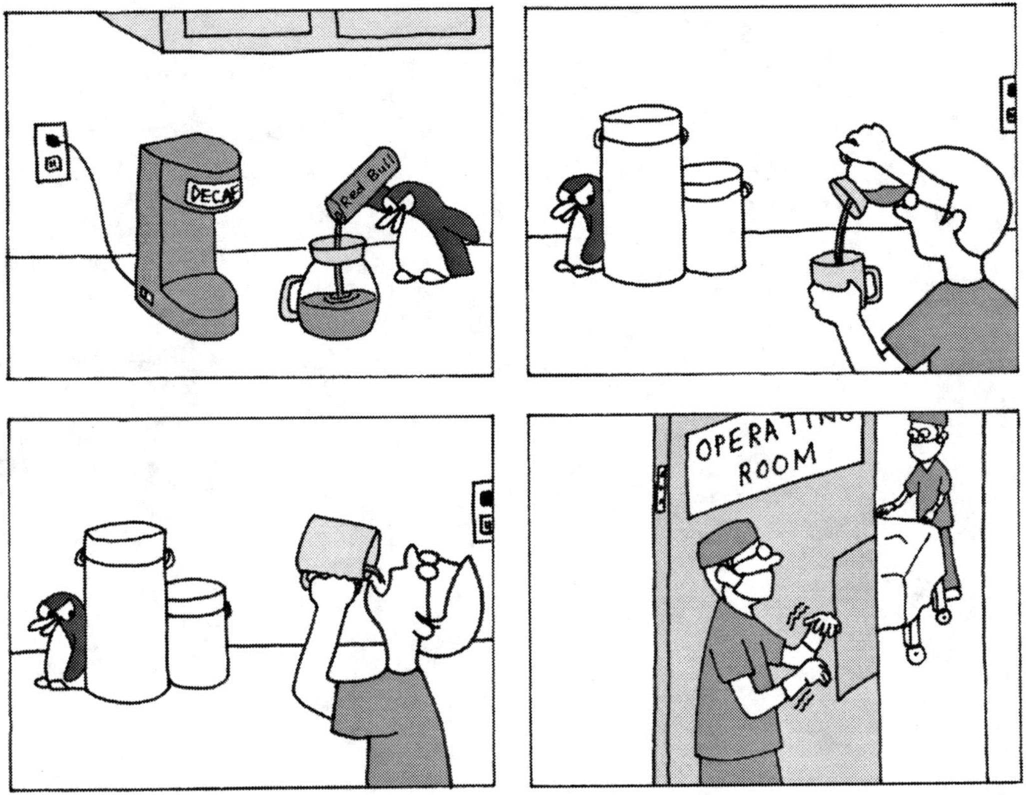
DECAF
Red Bull
OPERATING
ROOM

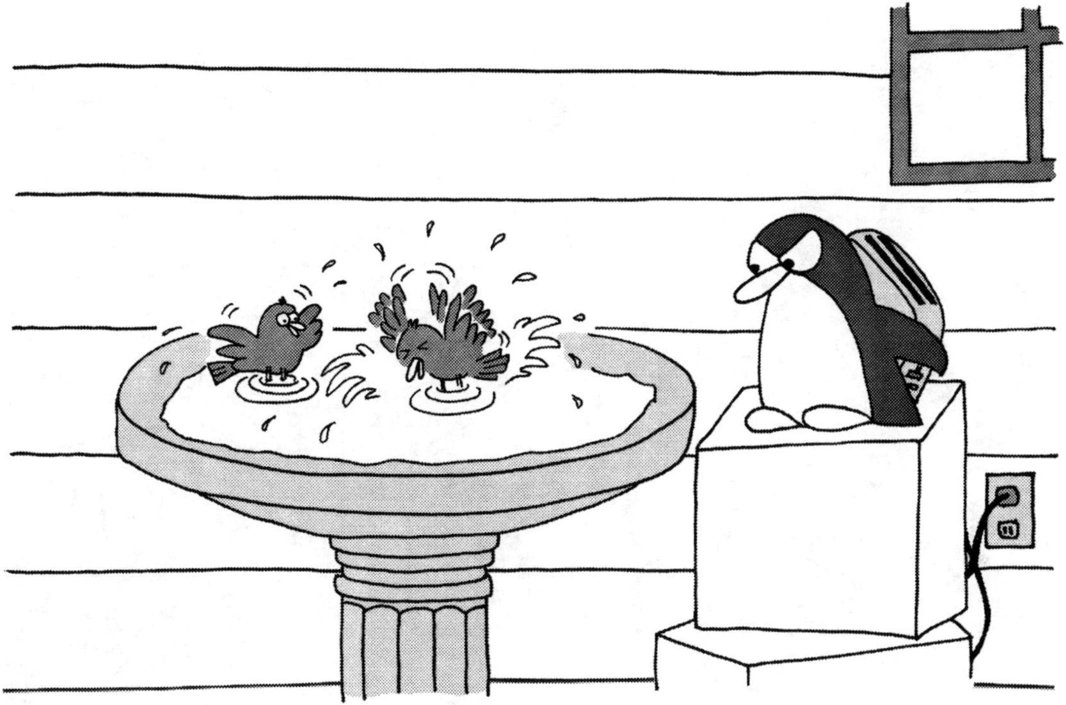

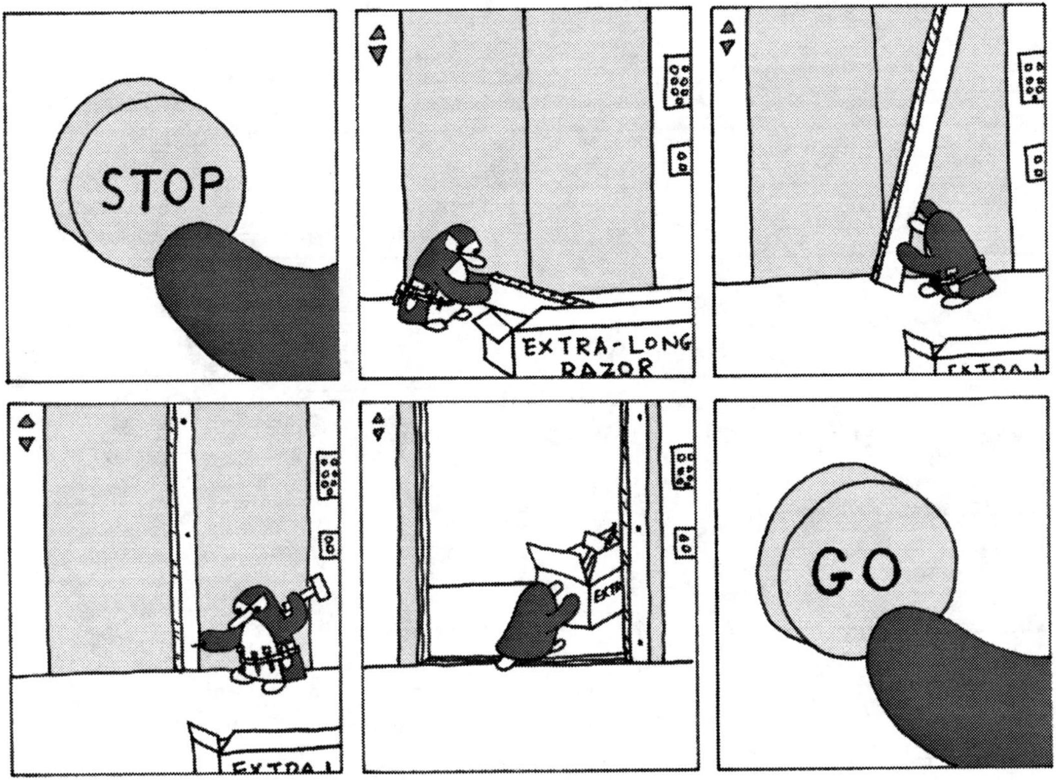
STOP
EXTRA-LONG
RAZOR
GO

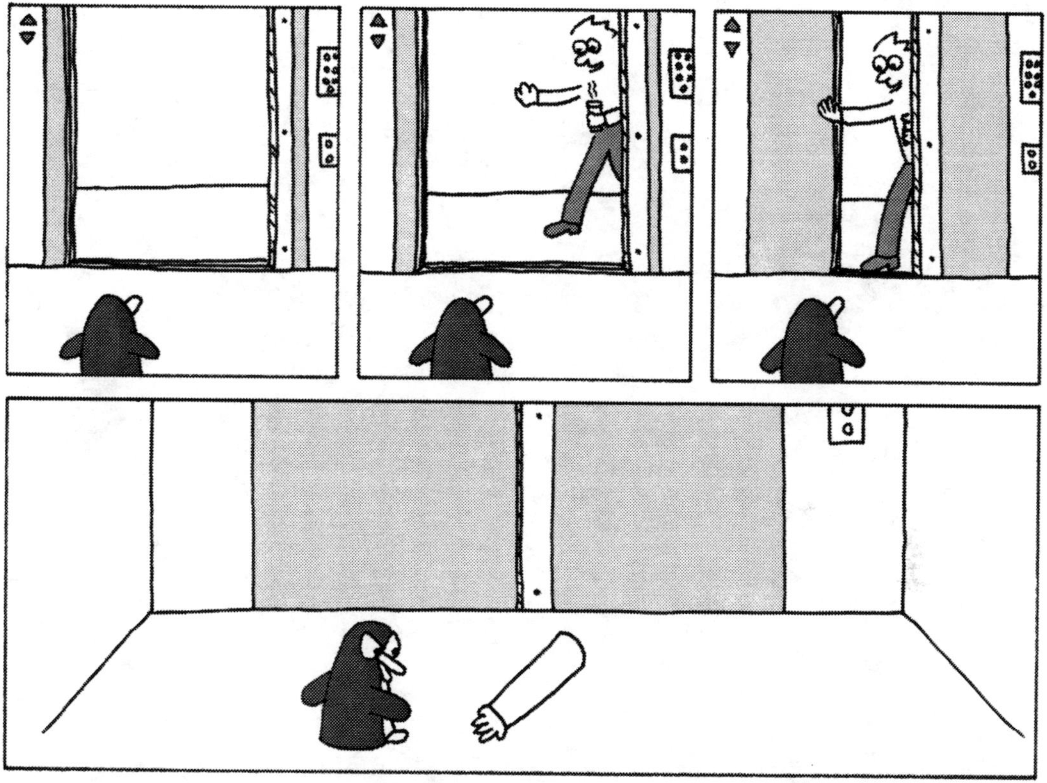

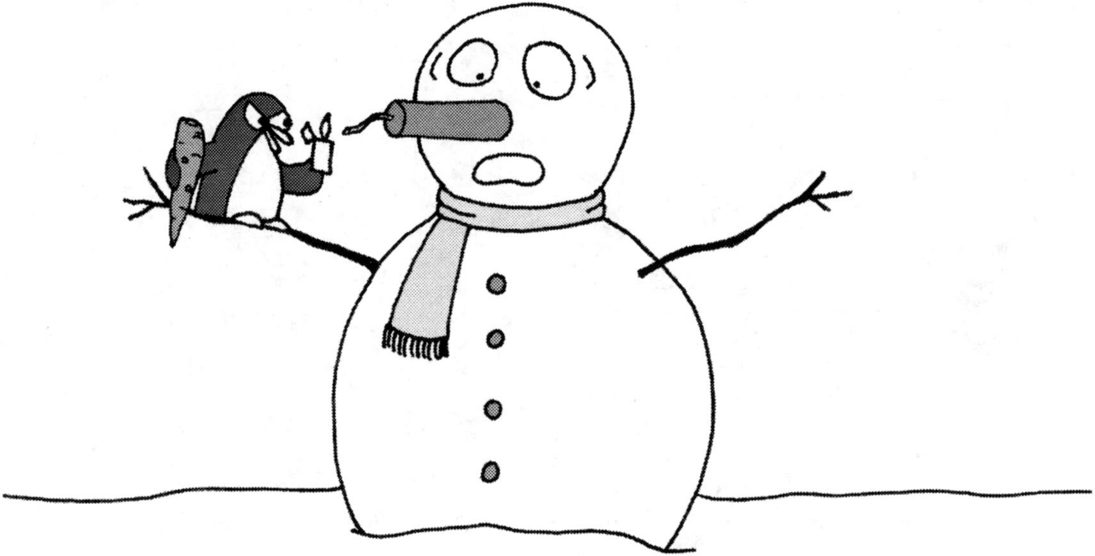

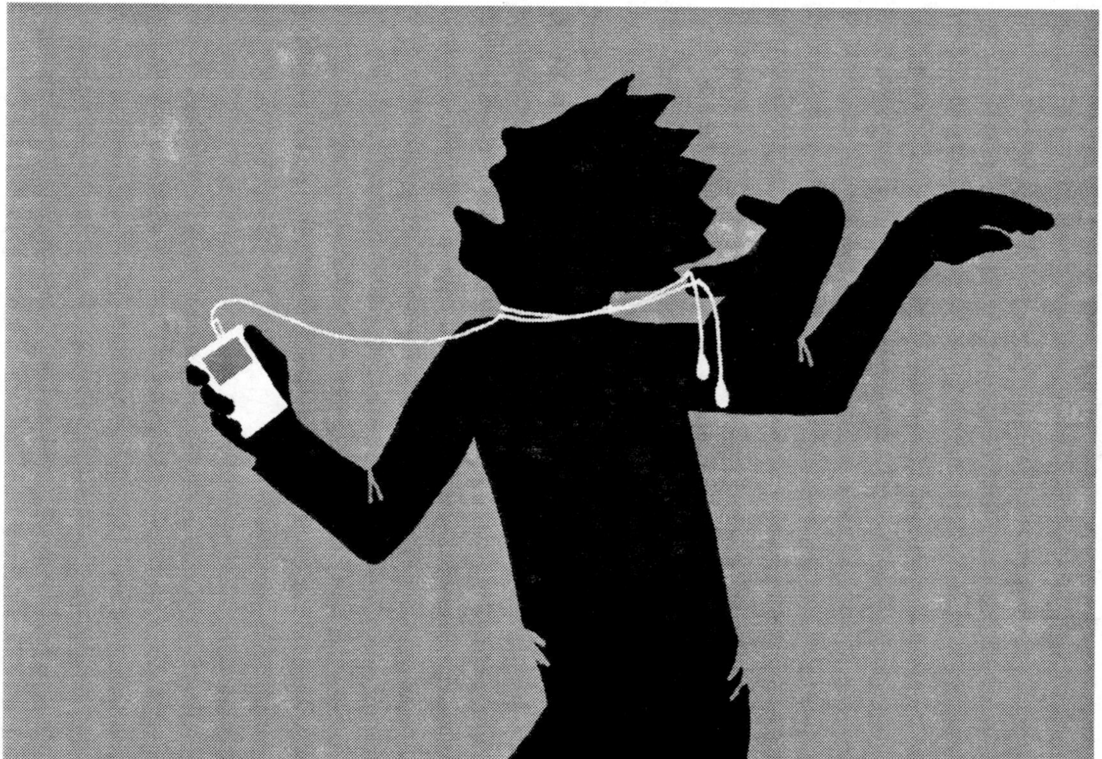

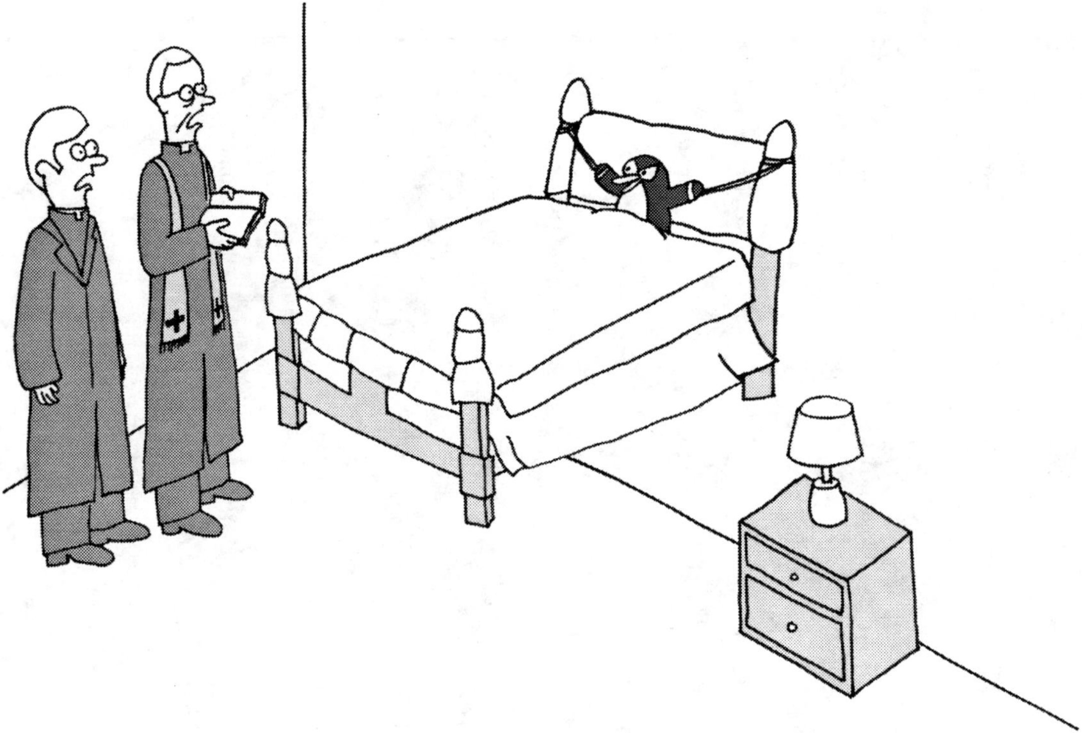

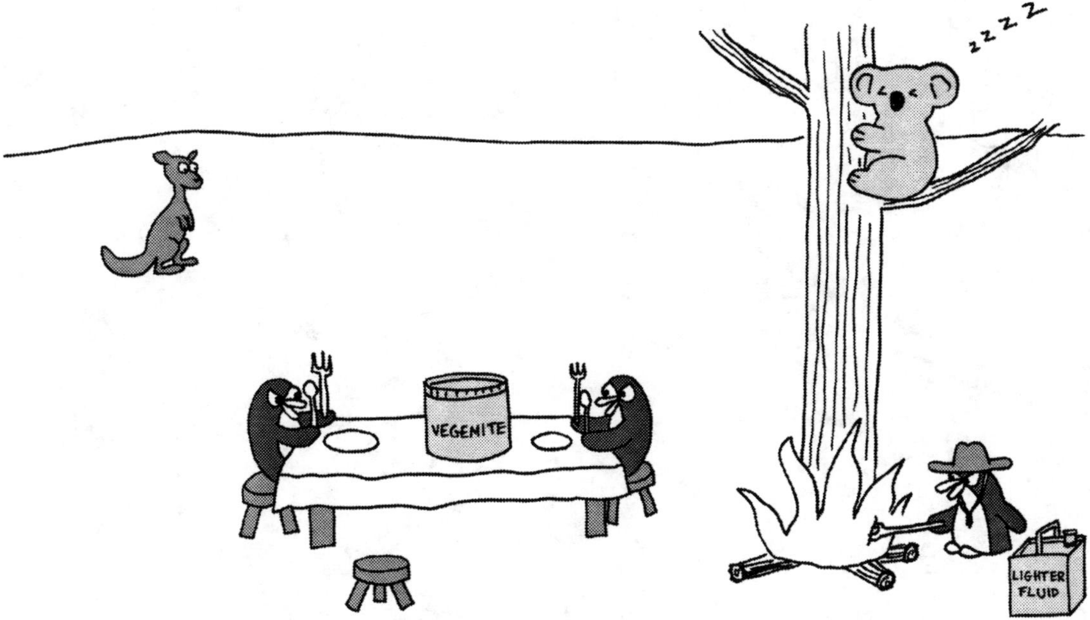
zzzz
VEGENITE
LIGHTER FLUID

KOALA ON THE BARBIE

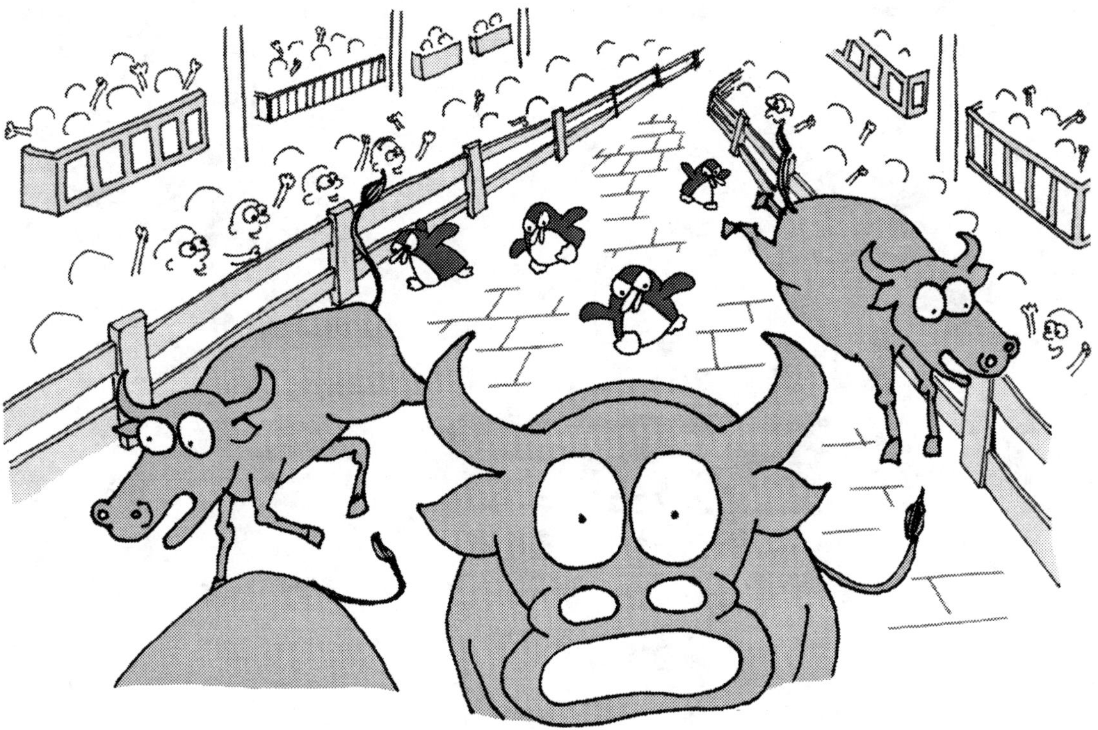

FERMILAB
PARTICLE ACCELERATOR
ATOM SMASHER
3000
ON
OFF

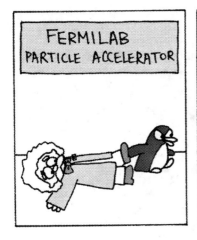

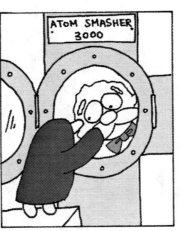

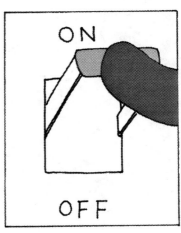

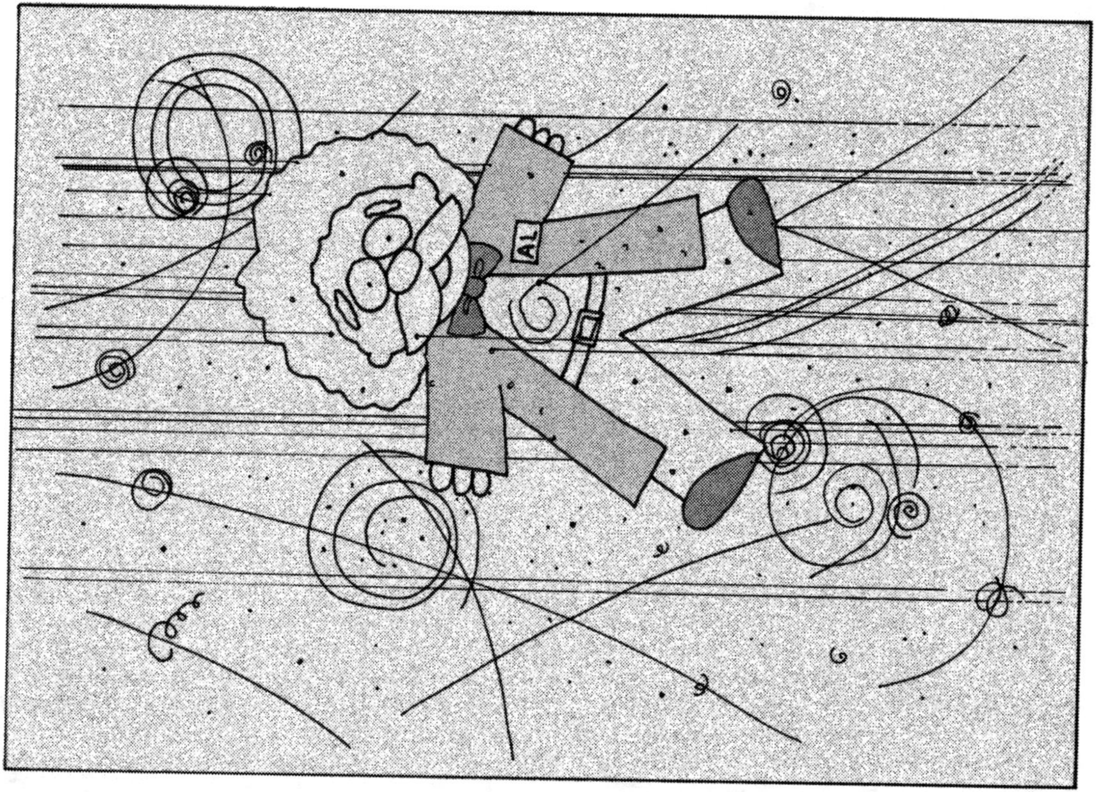
AL

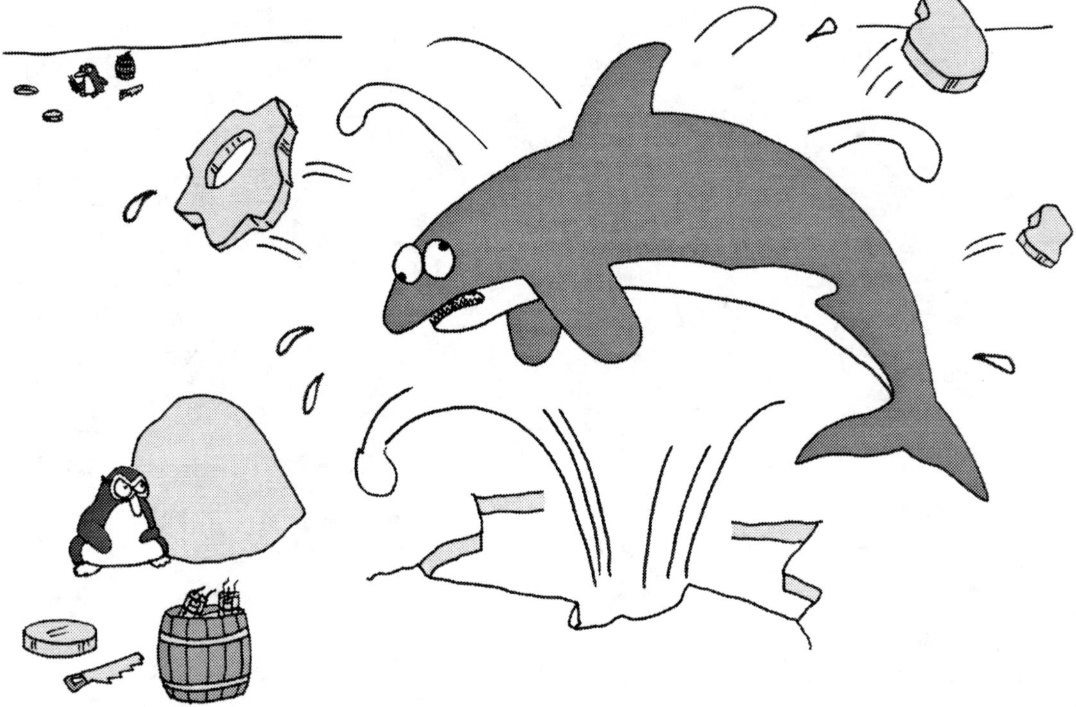

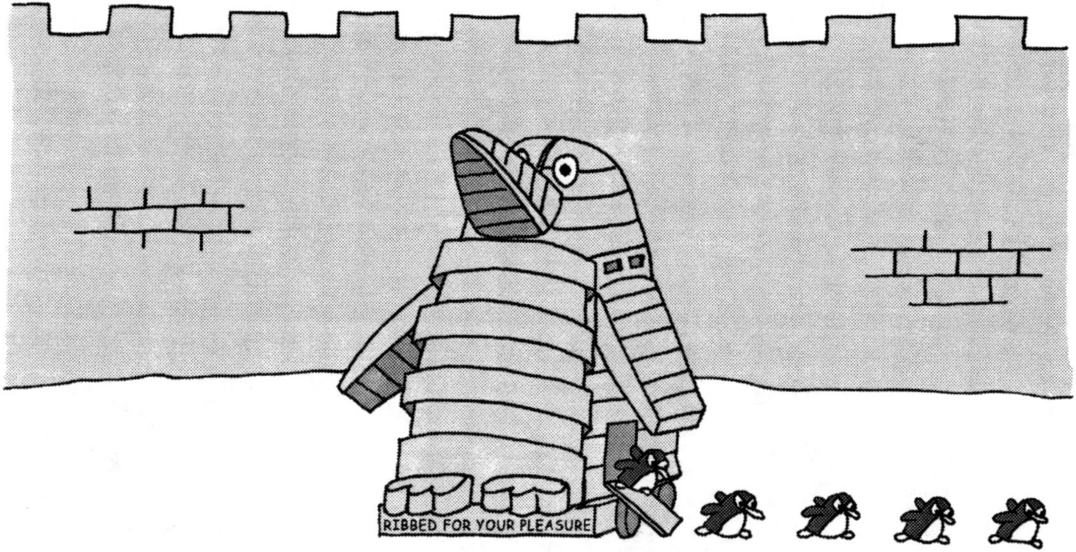
RIBBED FOR YOUR PLEASURE

TROJAN PENGUIN

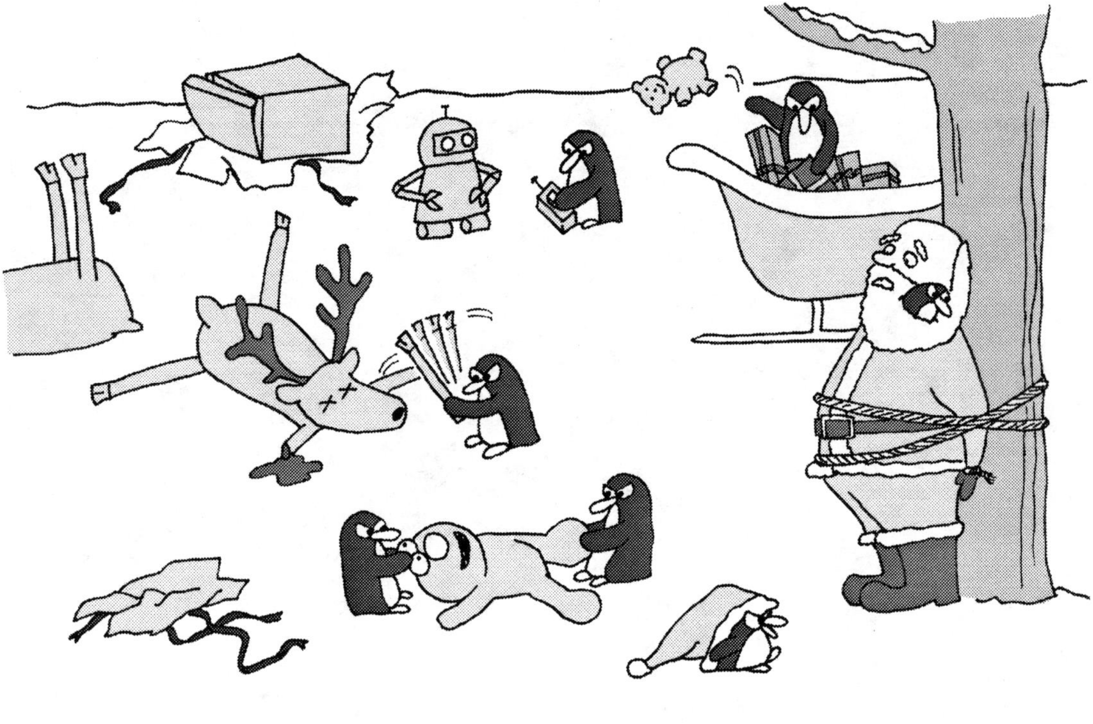

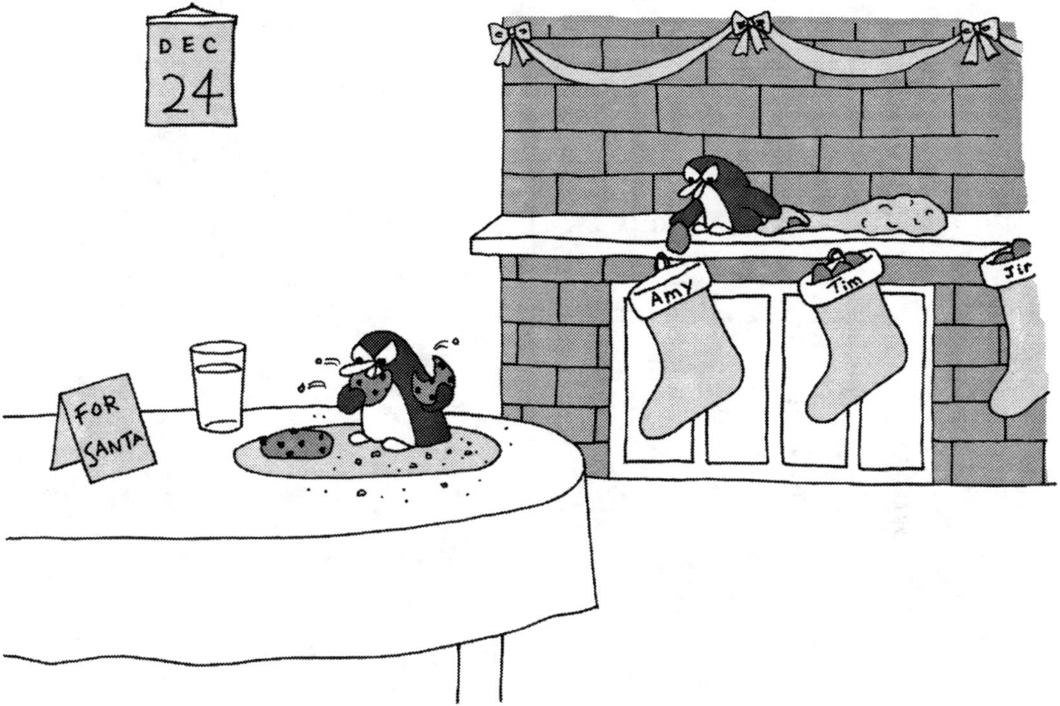
DEC
24
FOR SANTA
Amy
Tim

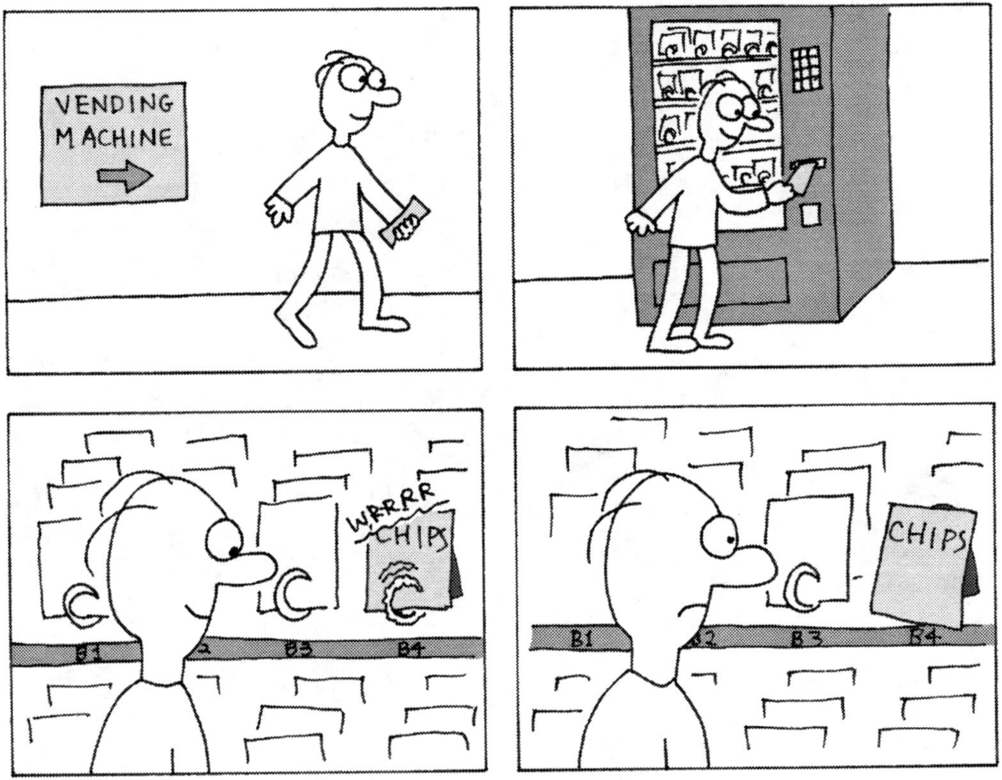
VENDING MACHINE
WRRRR
CHIPS
B1
B3
B4
B1
B2
B3
B4
CHIPS

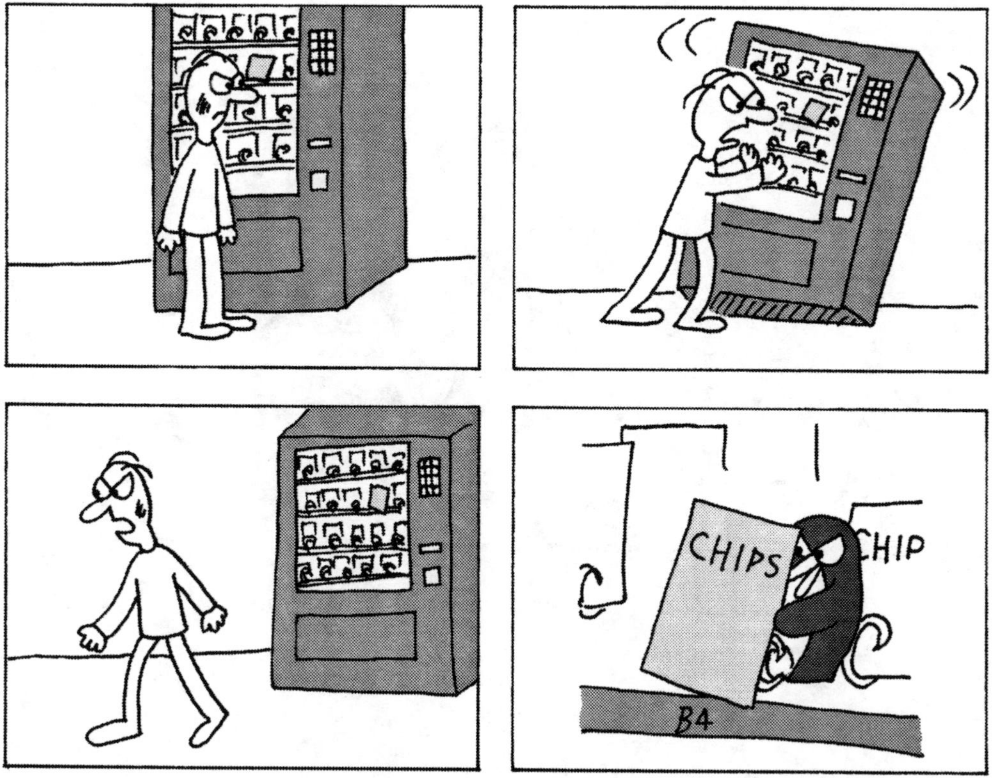
CHIPS
CHIP
B4

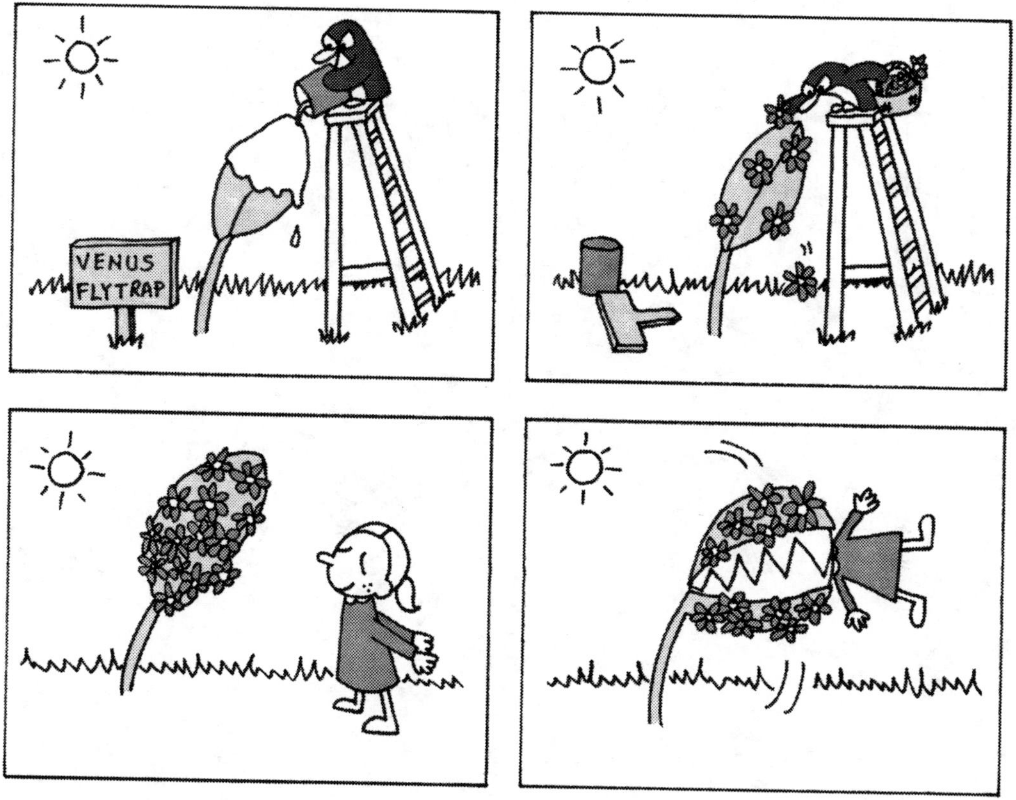
VENUS
FLYTRAP

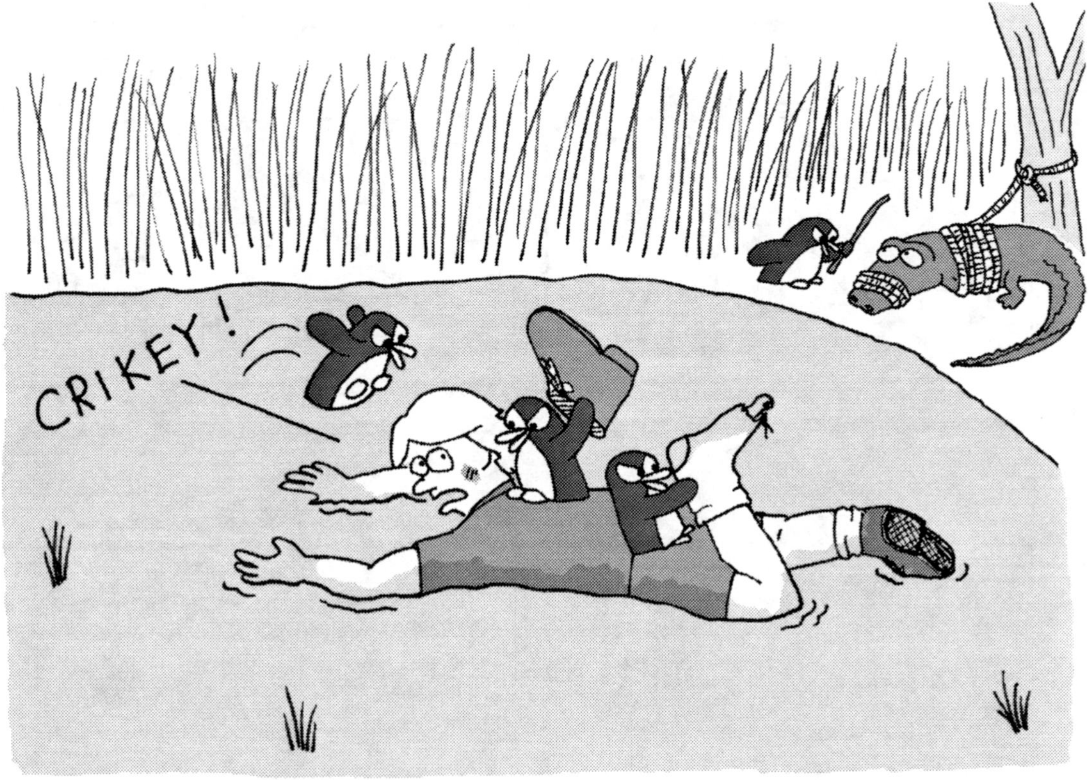
CRIKEY!

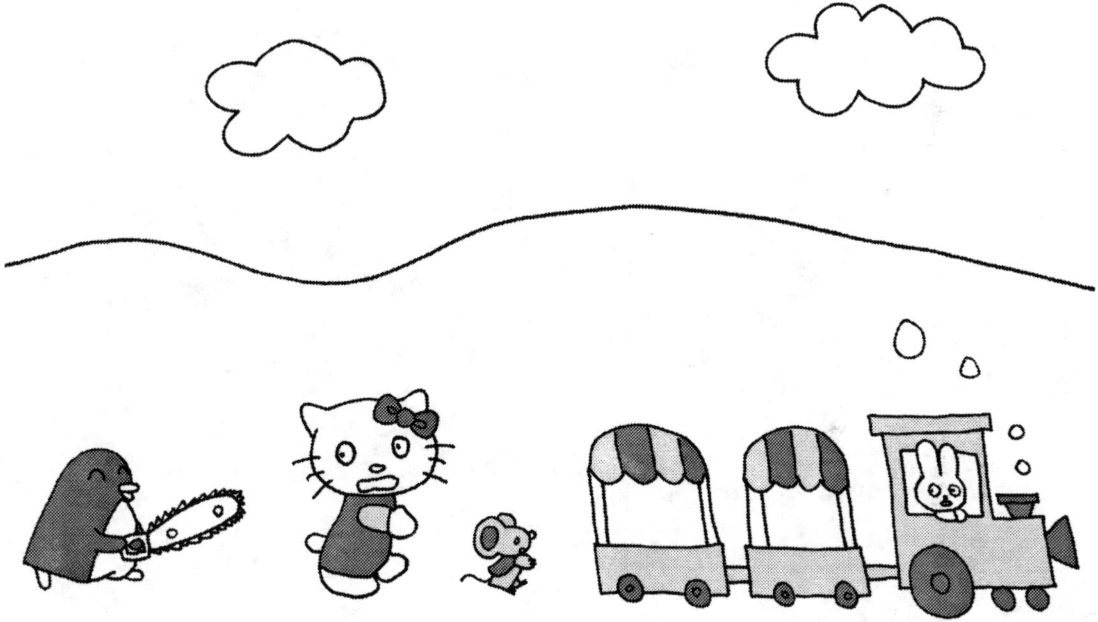

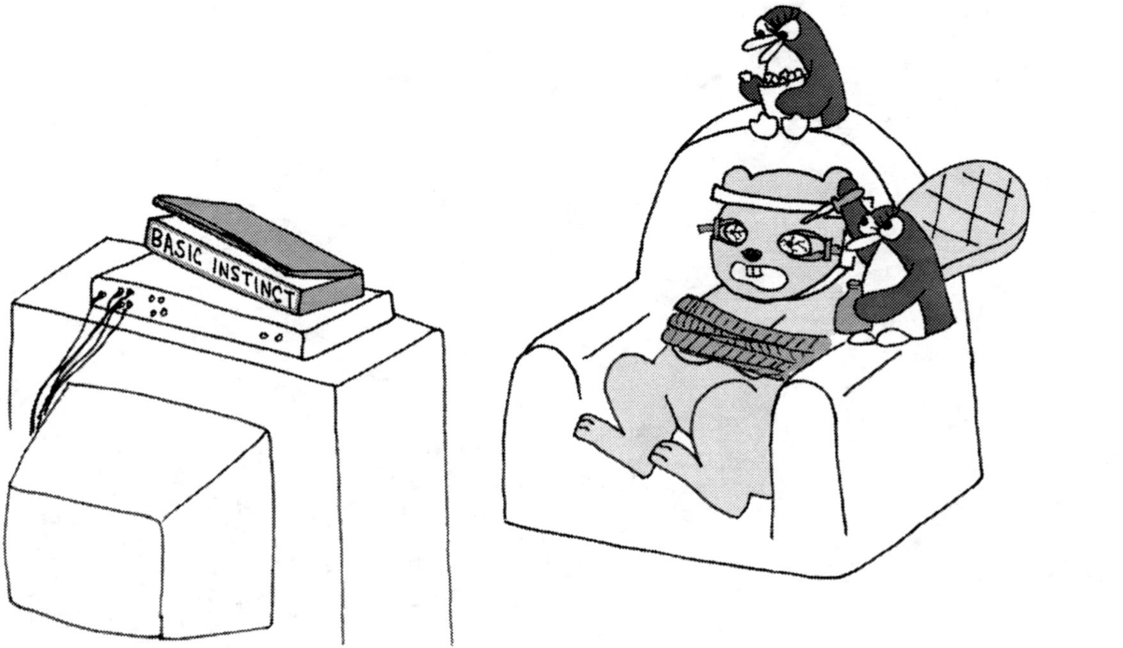
BASIC INSTINCT

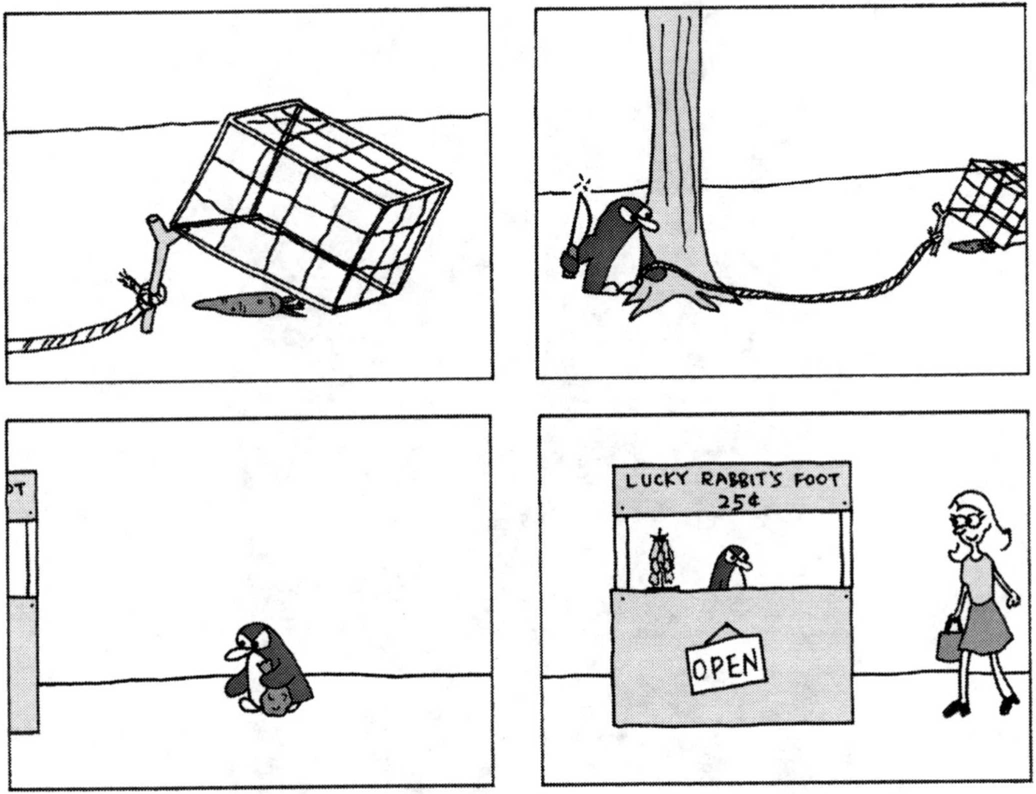

LUCKY RABBIT'S FOOT
25¢
OPEN

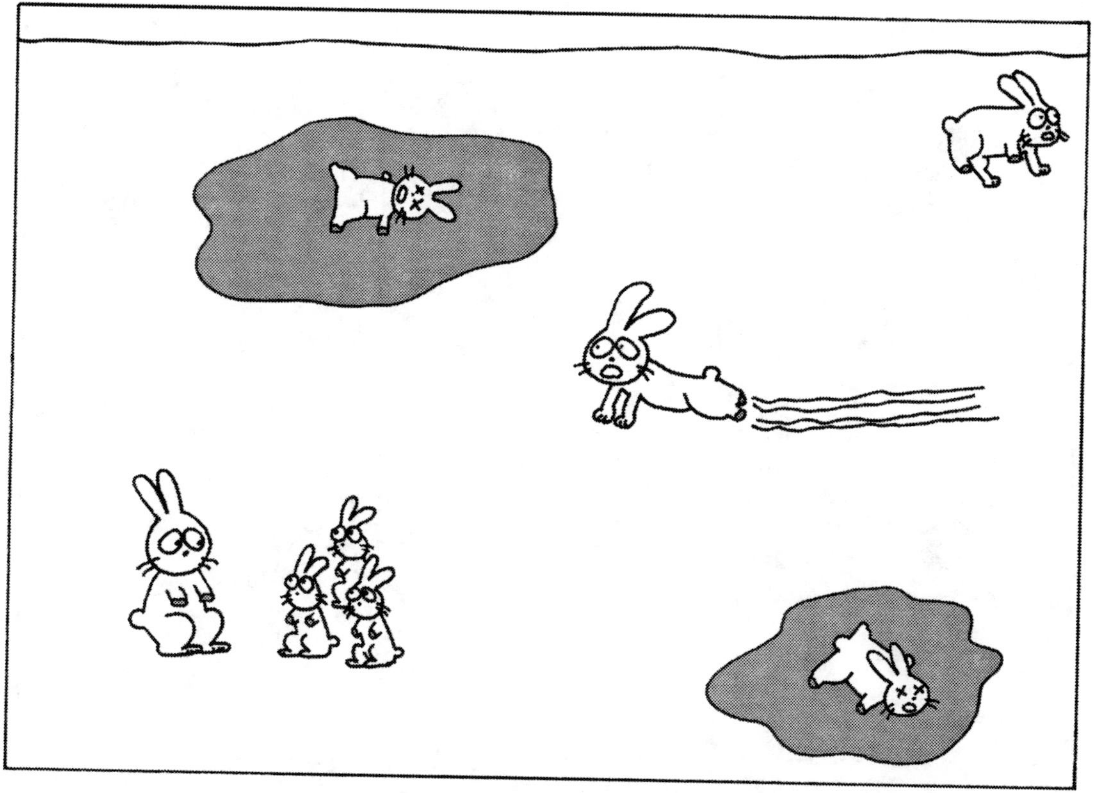

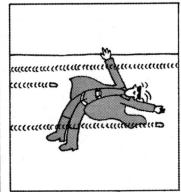

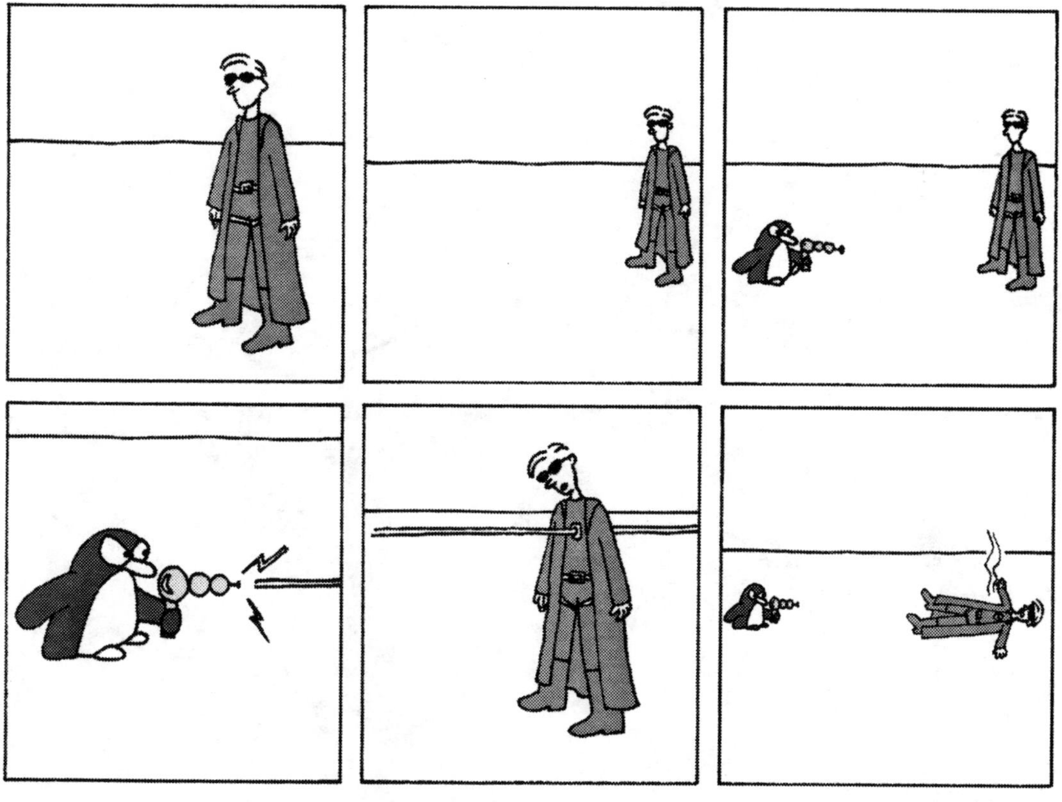

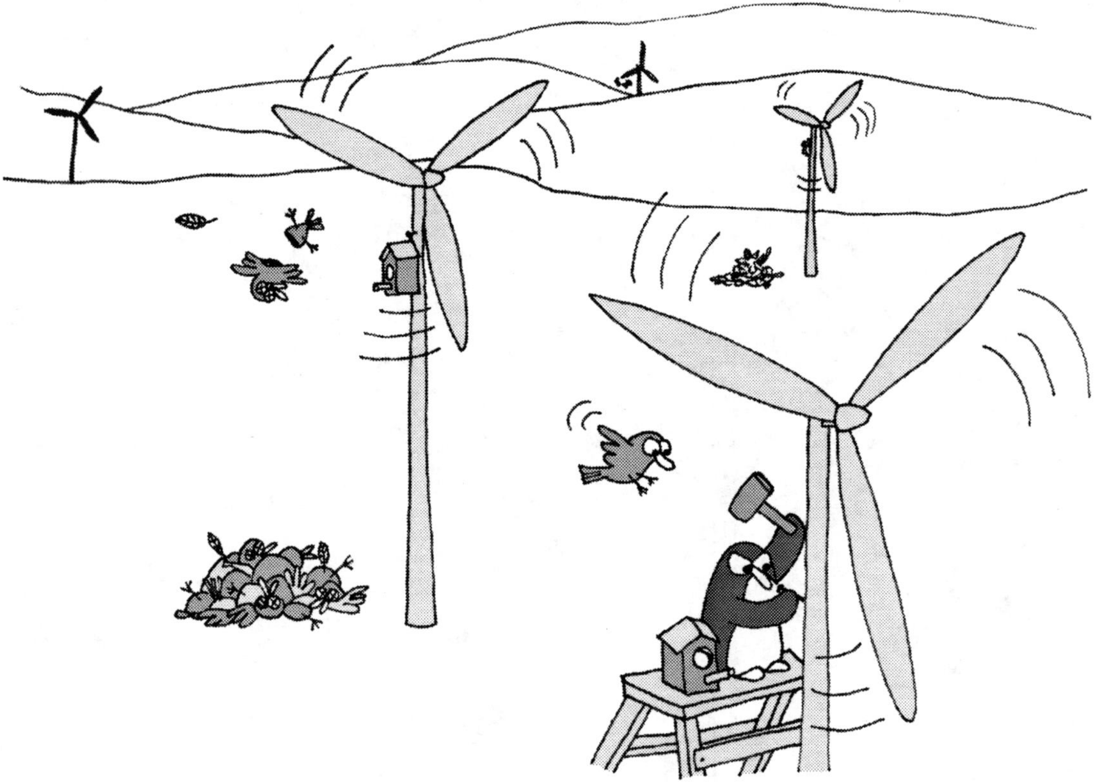

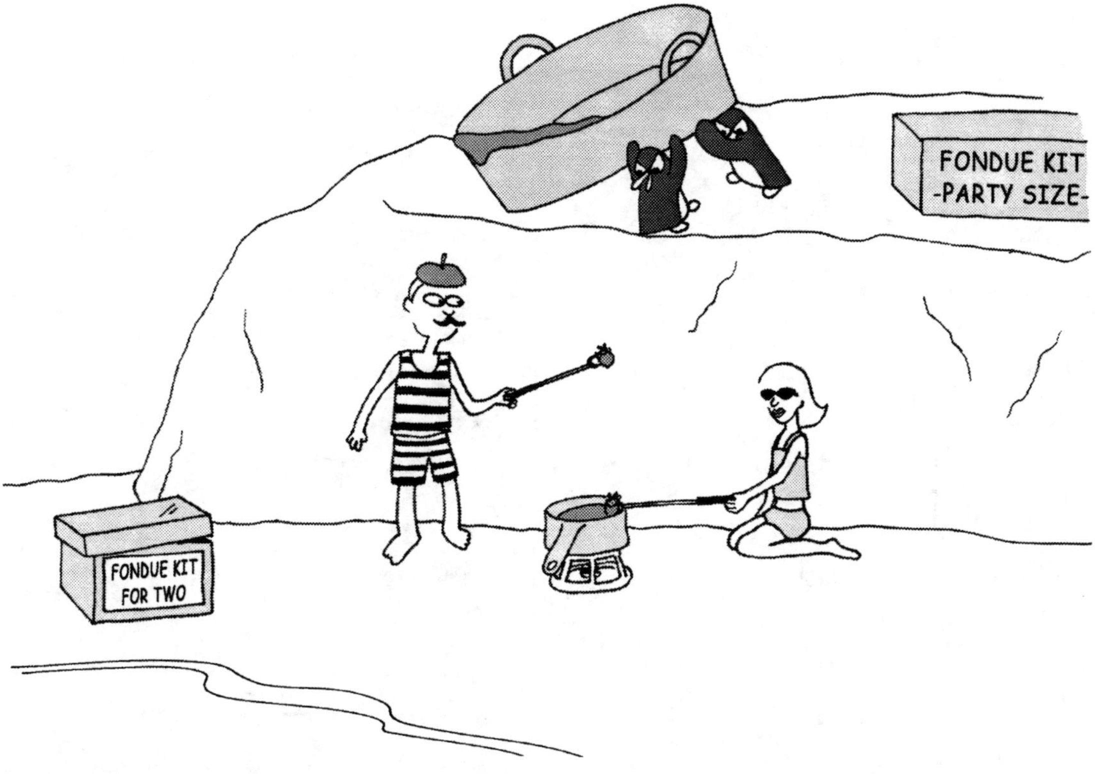
FONDUE KIT
-PARTY SIZE-
FONDUE KIT
FOR TWO

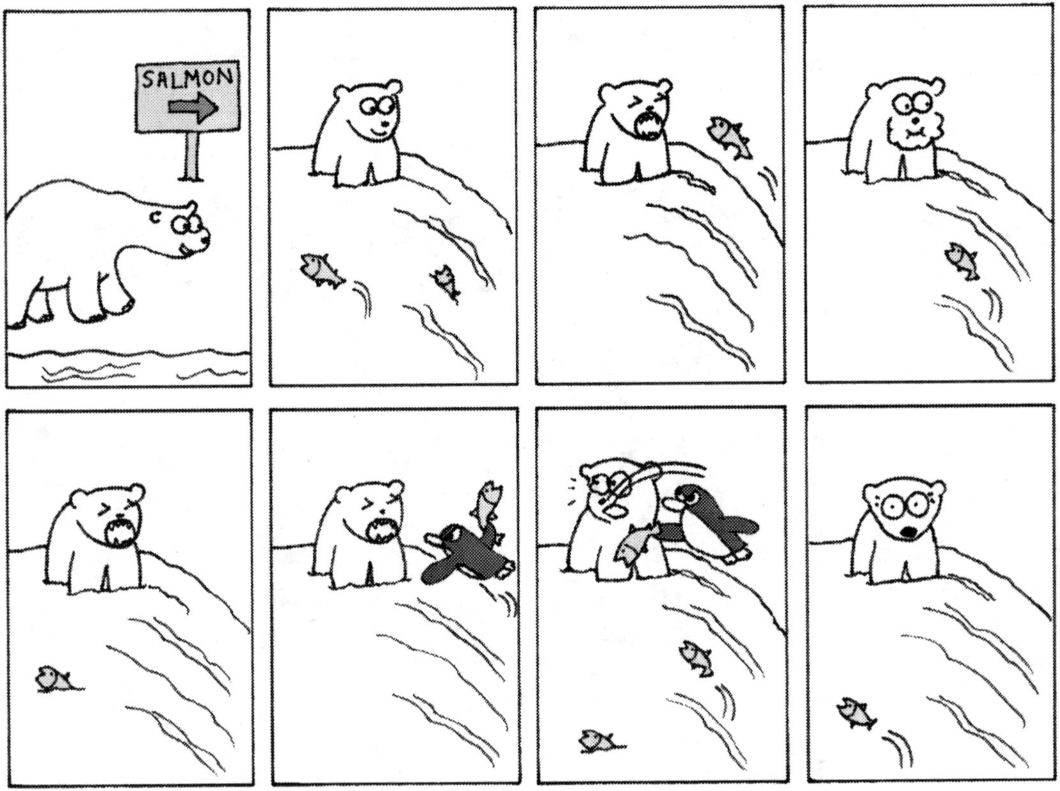
SALMON

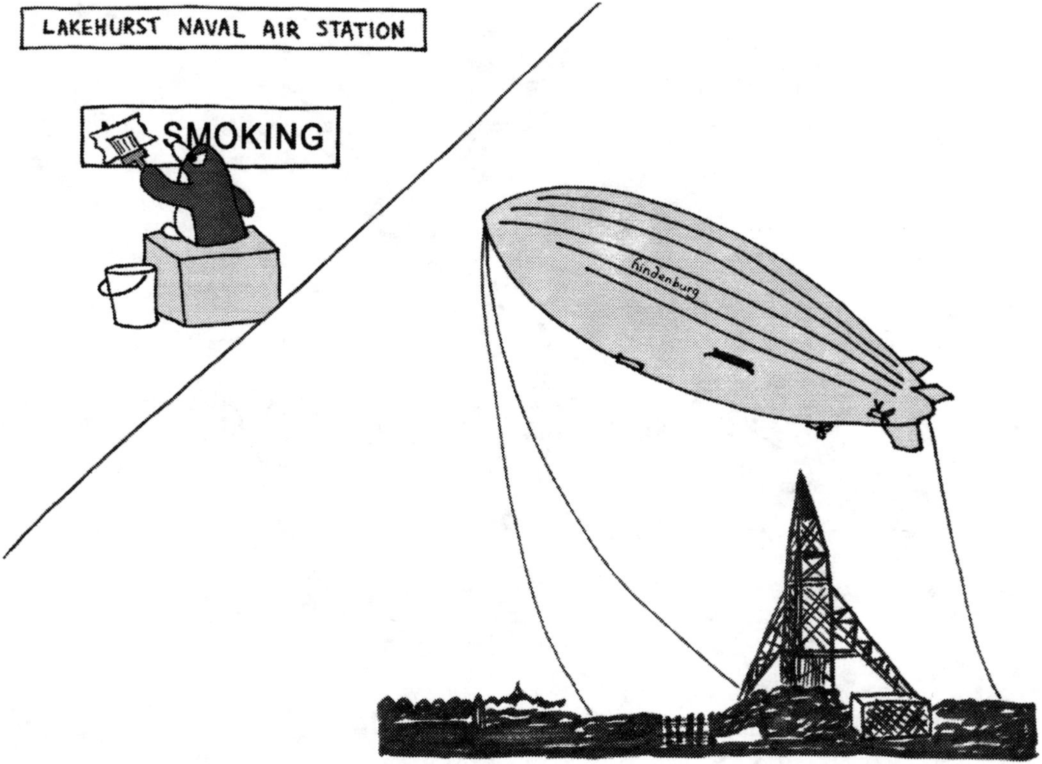
LAKEHURST NAVAL AIR STATION
SMOKING
Hindenburg

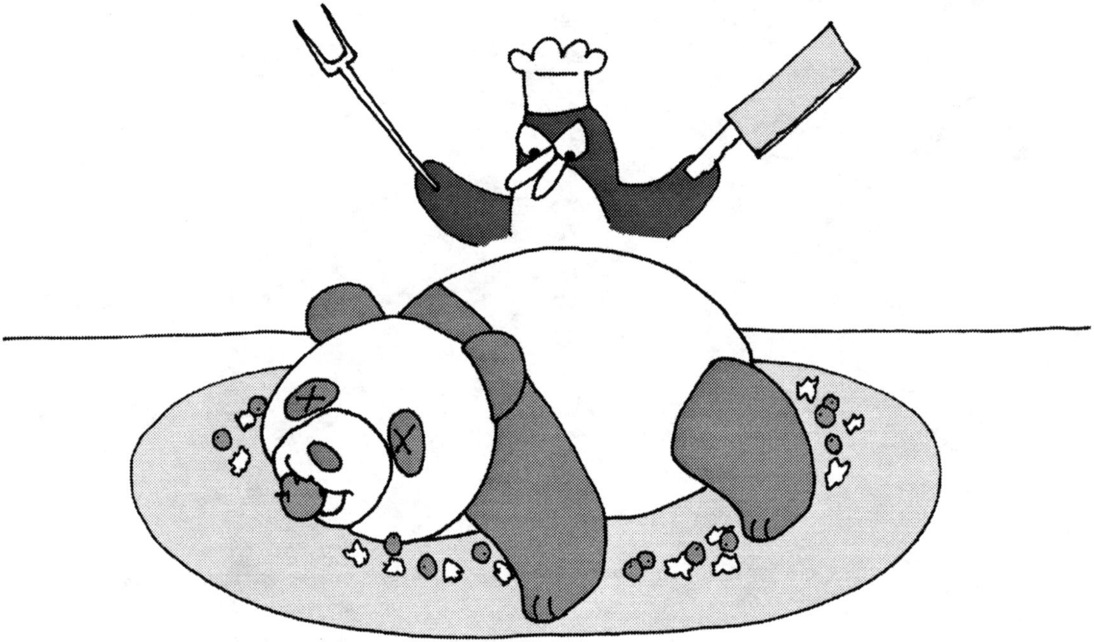

PEKING PANDA (ORDER 24 HRS IN ADVANCE)

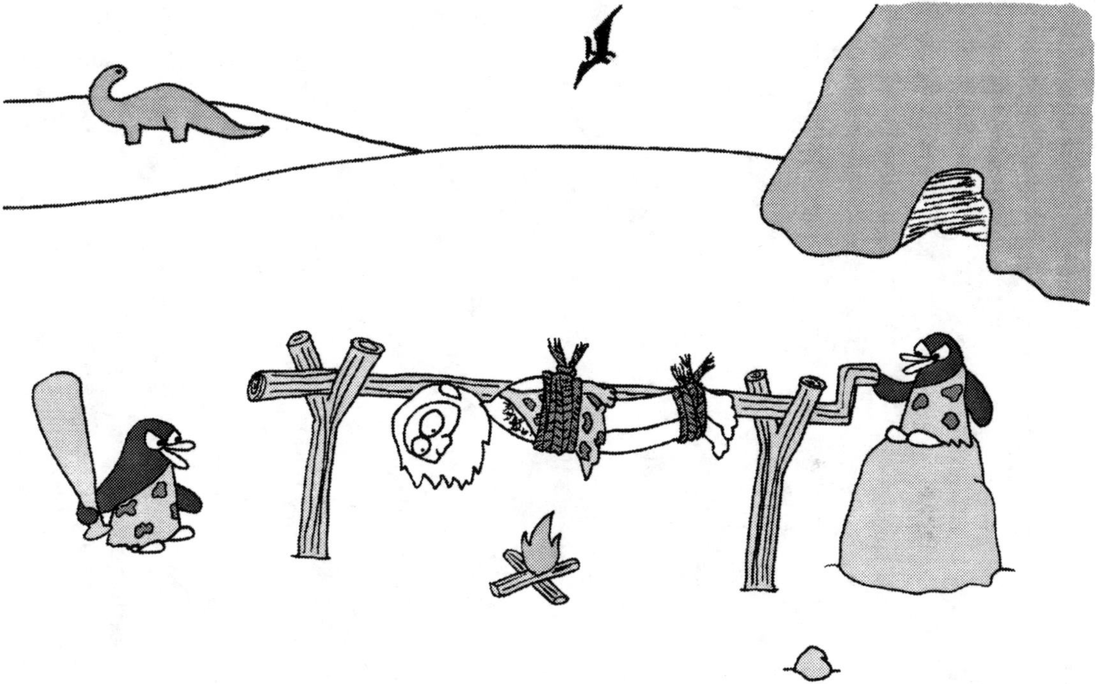

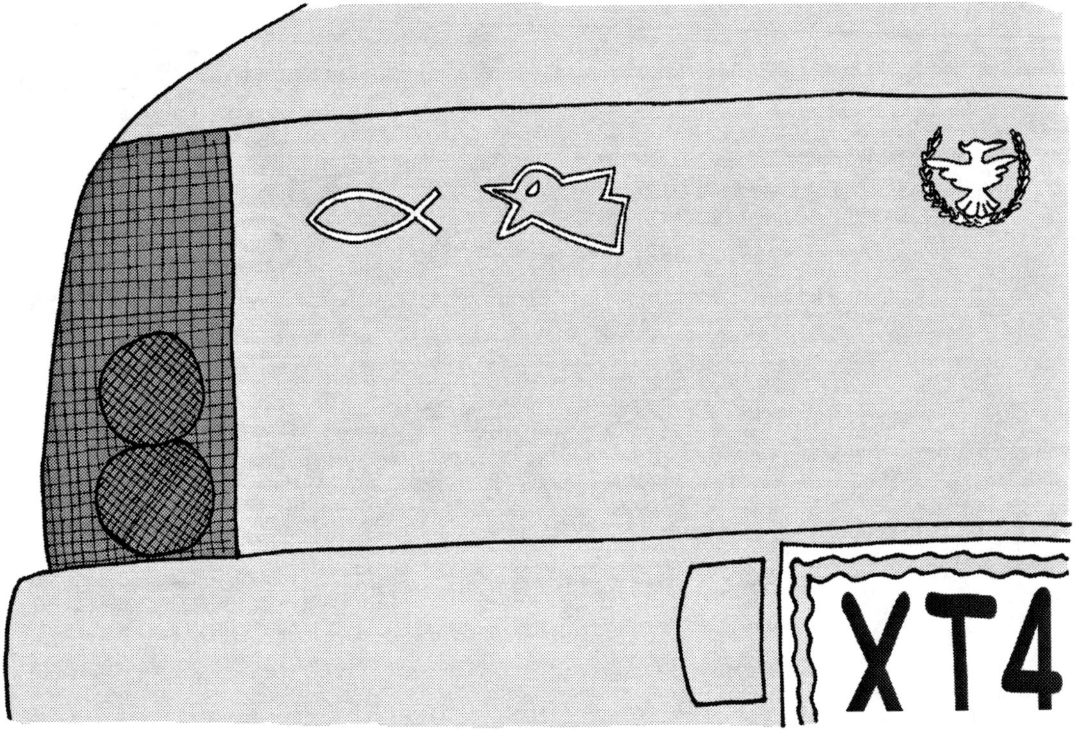
XT4

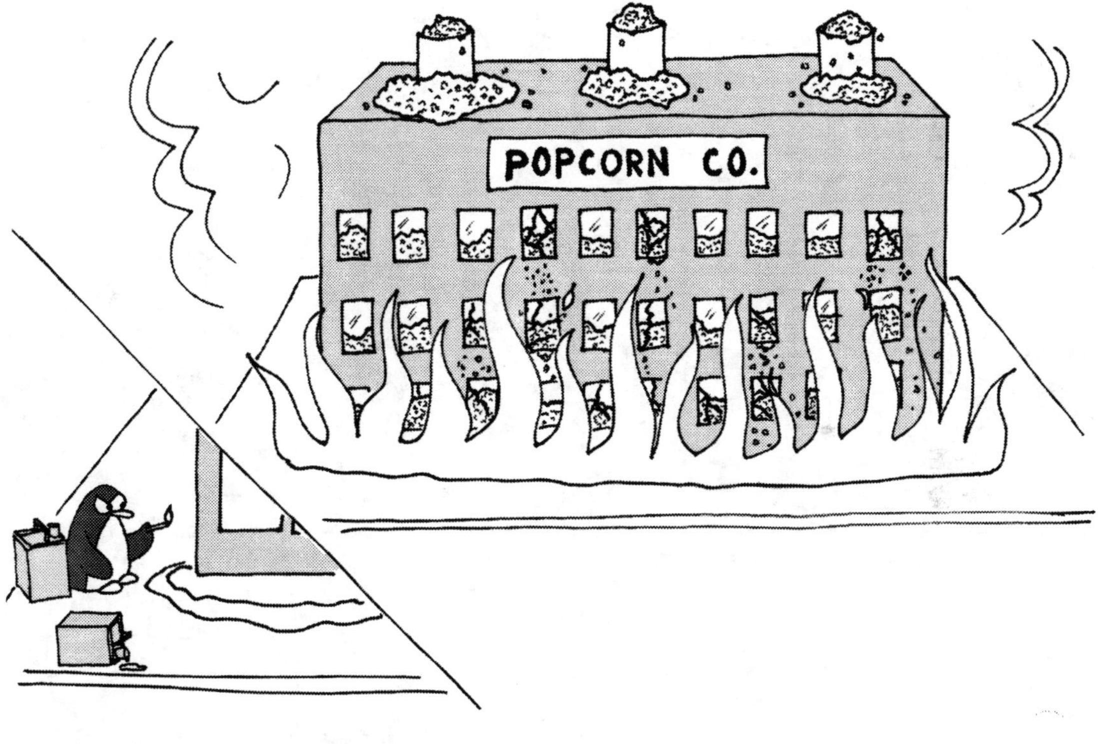
POPCORN CO.

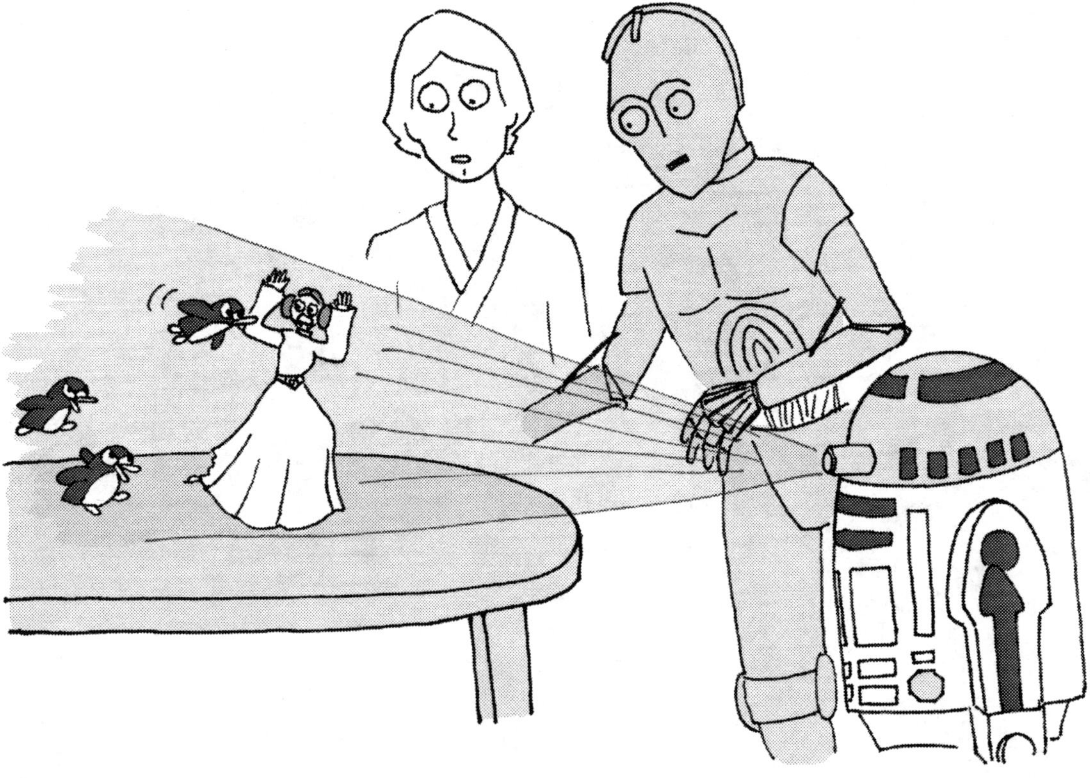

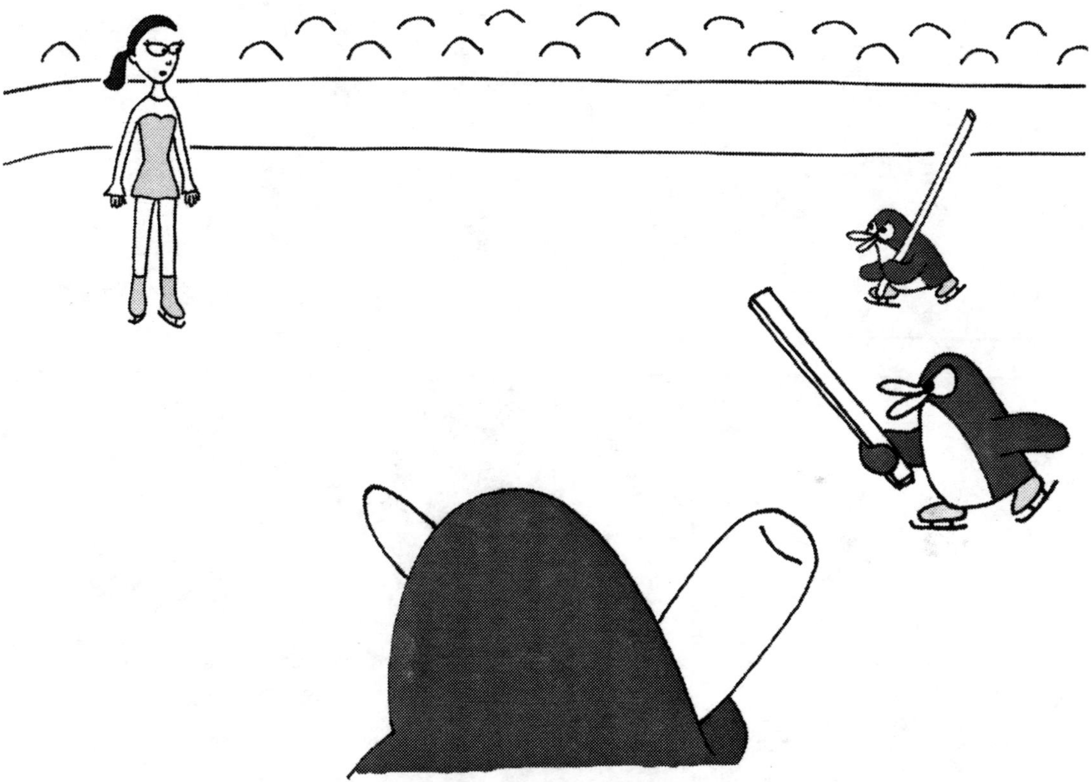

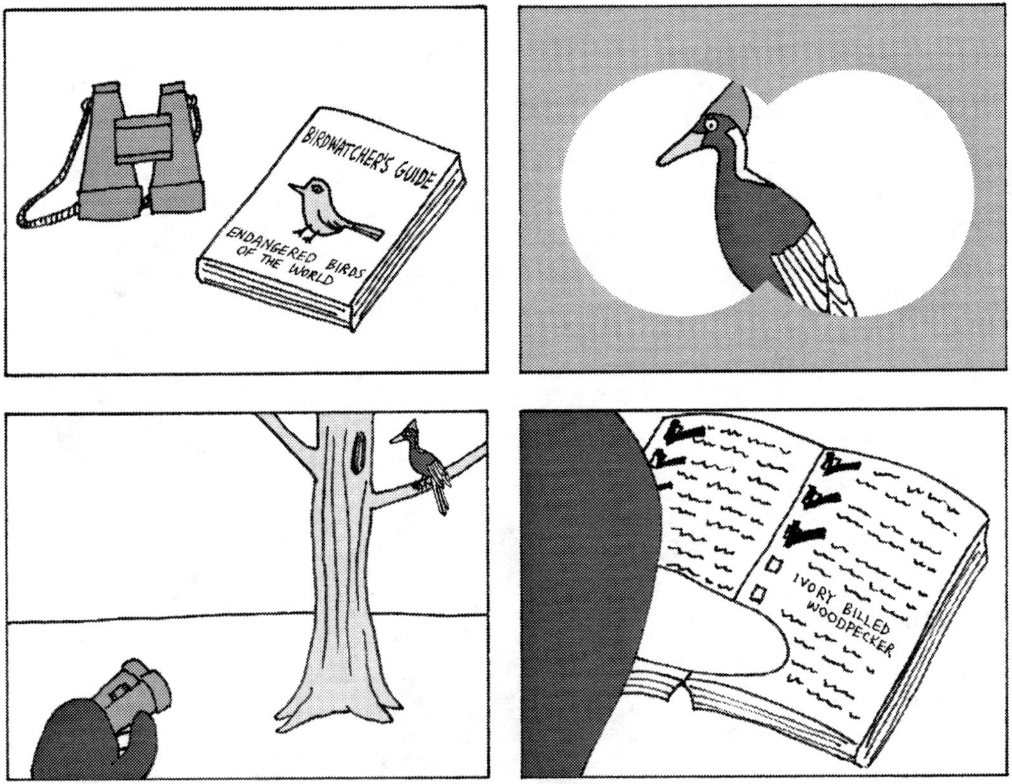
BIRDWATCHER'S GUIDE
ENDANGERED BIRDS OF THE WORLD
IVORY BILLED WOODPECKER

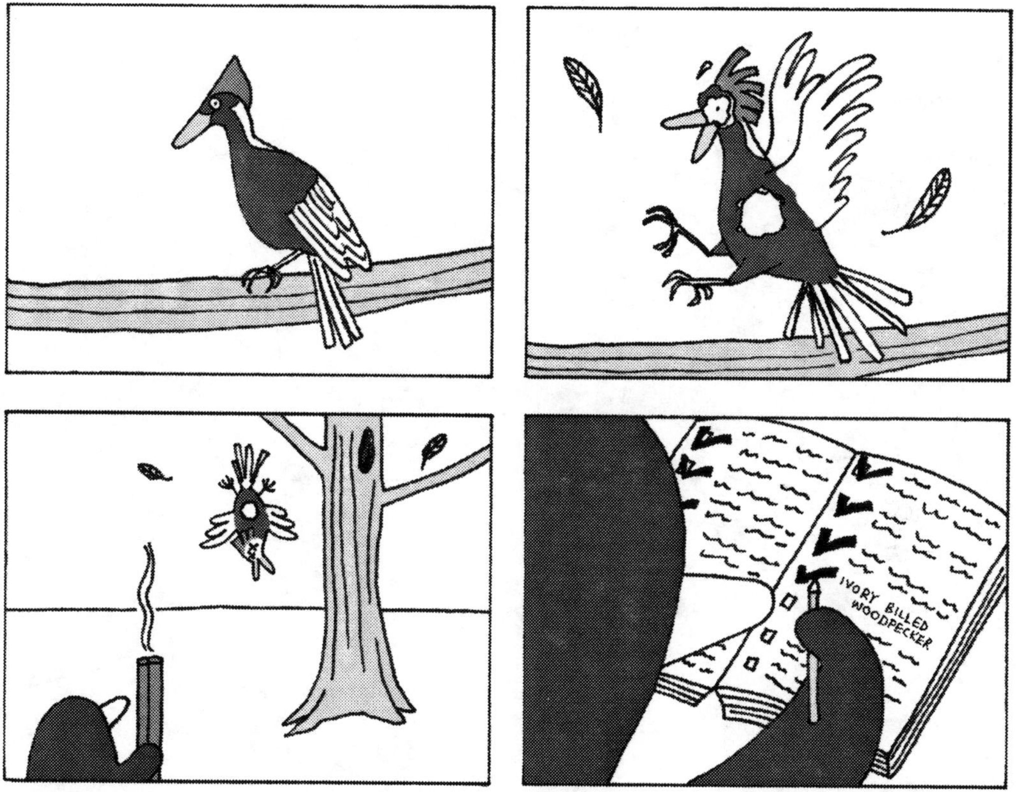
IVORY BILLED WOODPECKER

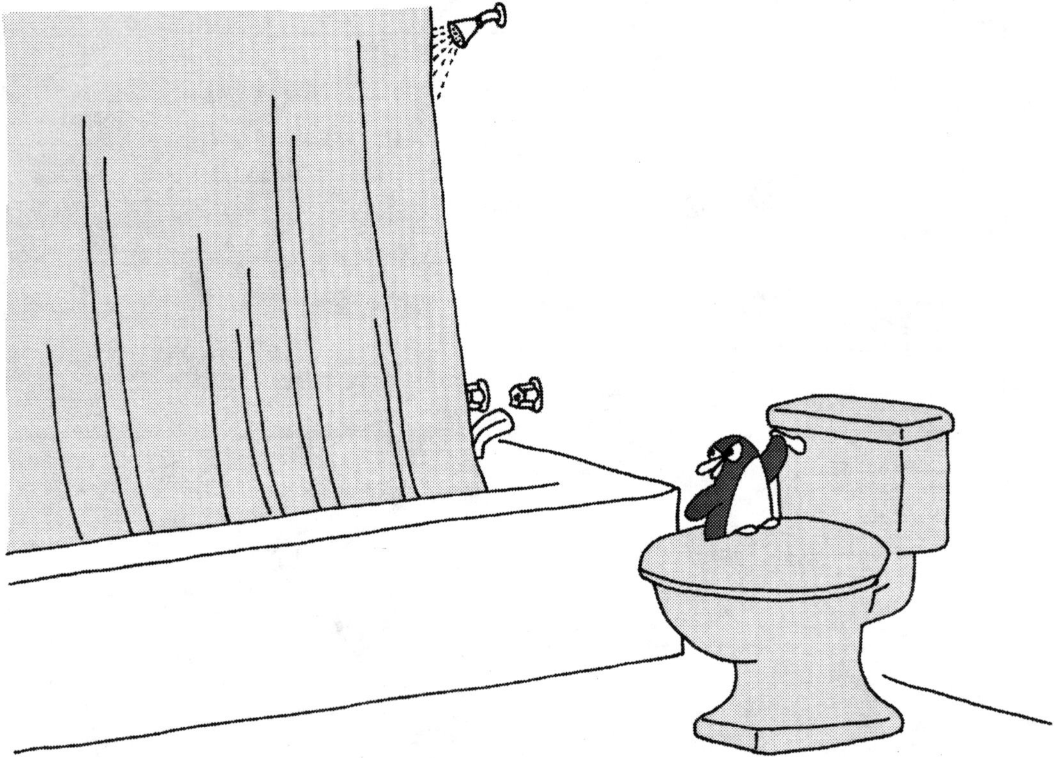

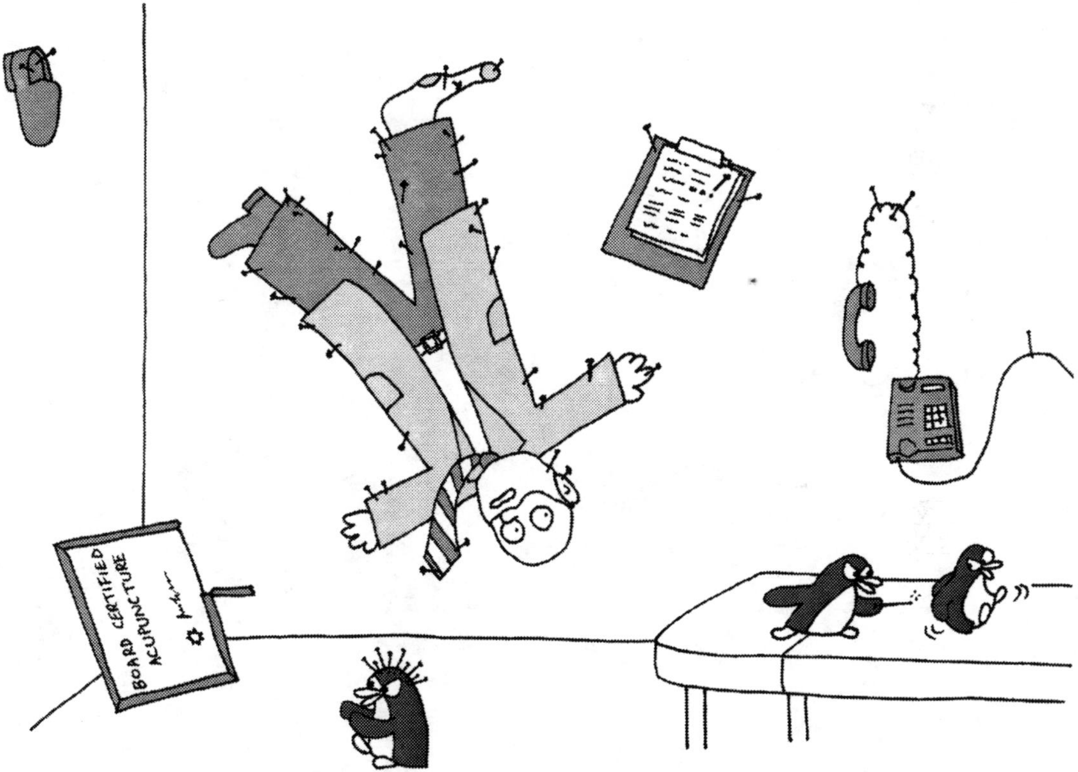
BOARD CERTIFIED
ACUPUNCTURE

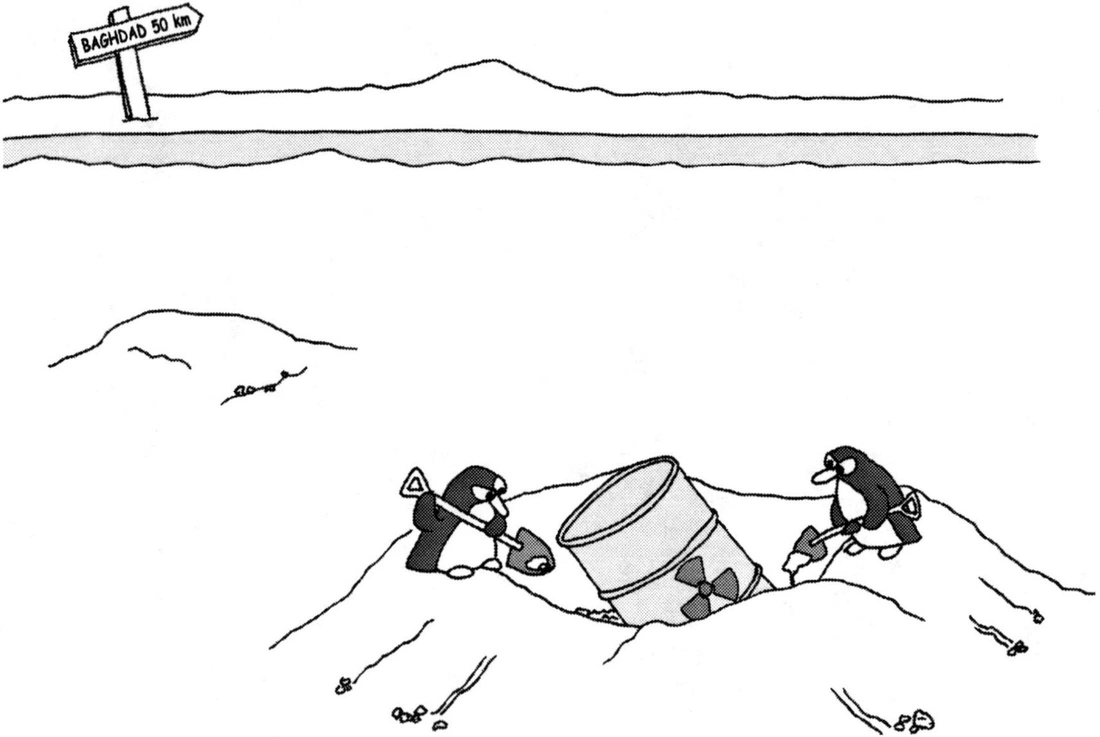
BAGHDAD 50 km